William Turberville

The Triumph of Love

Poems

William Turberville

The Triumph of Love
Poems

ISBN/EAN: 9783337006518

Printed in Europe, USA, Canada, Australia, Japan

Cover: Foto ©Thomas Meinert / pixelio.de

More available books at **www.hansebooks.com**

THE TRIUMPH OF LOVE

THE TRIUMPH OF LOVE

POEMS

BY

WILLIAM TURBERVILLE

LONDON

KEGAN PAUL, TRENCH, TRÜBNER & CO. LTD.

PATERNOSTER HOUSE, CHARING CROSS ROAD

1894

LONDON:
PRINTED BY GILBERT AND RIVINGTON, LD.,
ST. JOHN'S HOUSE, CLERKENWELL ROAD, E.C

TO THE QUEEN.

Fond Mother of Imperial sons
   Who dwell in lands beyond thy sea,
Rejoice ! for see their toil-worn hands
   Are stretched in helpful love to Thee.

What if thy eldest son has torn
   Himself away from thine embrace !
Thou know'st that in his secret heart
   He proudly owns his royal race ;

And would if danger threatened thee
   Be foremost to defend thy cause,
For he was dandled on thy knee,
   And nurtured in thy righteous laws.

Blow then a trumpet blast to Heaven,
   And let the listening nations know,
Thine Empire, knit by bonds of love,
   Shall never fall to foreign foe.

Years back in ceaseless storms of War,
  Thou slew'st the Pirates of the Deep,
And now thy ships in safety ride,
  Let not new Pirates think we sleep.

Then thou wert Mistress of the Seas,
  Now thou art Mother of the World,
And nevermore whilst thou art strong
  Shall Justice from her throne be hurled.

CONTENTS.

HE THAT IS PURE;

OR

HAROLD AND LILIAN.

In Love,—Life : in Death,—Love.

Part I. The Meeting.

PRELUDE.

HE that is pure is lovelier than the rose
Or white-robed lily ; fairer than the close
Of evening, when the palette of the sun
Lets all the colours, intermingling, run
In fine confusion ; fresher than the morn
When shaking off Night's sensuous arms with
    scorn :
And far more precious than are strings of pearls
Encircling lily necks half hid with curls ;
And rarer than the frost in Summer's breath,
When in her sleep at night she dreams of Death ;

Than snow encircling her in sunny June,
Blanching her beauty in a deadly swoon :
Yet Purity the breath of Heaven distils
To cleanse all life ; with dewy drink it fills
The flowers and leaves and ruminating grass,
And lifts their odours to us as we pass
In the first sunbeams ; and the Sea's voice roars
In gladness as it nervously outpours
The purifying essence of its salt
Beneath the clear Heaven's telescopic vault
Of purest blue ; so, too, the bustling Wind
Disperses death-airs when the world has sinned
Against the laws of health ; and then again,
The land is cleansed by purifying Rain ;
And pestilence is vaporized away,
In the consuming Fire of the Day.

If then fair Nature purifies its forms
In the electric glory of its storms,
Is it not meet that in man's heart's domain
The storms of mighty Love should cleanse each
　　　stain,
And purify the thoughts that now corrode
The young man's life who scorns the moral code ?
To this end let me tell a simple tale
Of Purity all soiled and sorrow-pale.

LILIAN'S COUNTRY LIFE.

Fair Lilian lived beneath the Southwold skies
A maid of beauty ; virtue from her eyes
Laughed forth with each inflection of her mind,
Full of true knowledge, of a lovelier kind
Than comes from mere delight in printed books ;
She knew the shyest flower's secret nooks,
And where a bird would hide its love-born nest
Far from that strange inquisitorial pest
We mis-name Man, (who should a saviour be,
And not the harsh destroyer that we see).
She knew, too, all the wonders of the sun,
And loved to ponder on that Glorious One
Who poised it in the blue ; she watched its rays
Entice the snowdrop to peep forth and praise
Its Maker ; and she heard the snowdrop tell
The slender crocus to come out as well ;
Till one by one the flowers dressed in green
Covered the nude Earth with a painted screen.
She watched the insects, too, come forth to play
In the warm comfort of a sunny day,
But never bee or any creeping thing,—
However treacherous its painful sting—
Hurt Lilian ; she was too good and kind,—
And all these living things knew Lilian's mind.
She felt, too, all the glories of the moon,

Its crescent coyness changing all too soon
Through full-orbed splendour into black disdain,
Hiding its beauty till it smile again ;
But then her thoughts would nestle in the stars
In happy dreams with Venus or with Mars,
(As though they were real persons in the skies,
And fit companions for a maid so wise,)
And yet, with all this love of flower and tree
And peerings out into infinity,
She loved domestic virtues quite as well,
And was distressed if e'er mishap befell
The household duties ; never has a maid
With finer virtues on this dull earth strayed,
But, best of charms that maidens can possess,—
She lived unconscious of her loveliness.

Southwold bloomed over England's Eastern sea,
A lovely spot : its sun-born greenery
Crept down its sloping cliffs and almost kissed
The fondling waves, which oft-times surged and
   hissed
In desperation to embrace it more,
But the pale moon looked down and hushed its
   roar,
And cooled its swelling love with jealous eye,
Lest its rude wooing might produce a sigh
Throughout the land. as in the distant past

When wealthy Dunwich in its arms was cast
And lost for ever ; Lilian often thought
Of its fair homes to desolation brought
By the bewitching sea she loved so well ;
And sometimes she would picture 'neath its
    swell
The buried city, busy as of yore,
With Love for ever opening Mercy's door,
And Hate as often charging Love away :
Thus would she image fancies grave and gay,
As she her skiff sailed through the dancing waves
And o'er the long-forgotten Dunwich graves.

And down by Walberswick an abbey rare
Spread out its ruined life ; Lilian would there
Endow the land with visions of romance,
Hear trumpets blowing dooms, and see the glance
Of spear and sword, like cruel glittering eyes,
Spread fear around ; and she would bid uprise
The ruined walls, which her fond mind regraced
With Gothic ornaments all deftly chased
On pillar, groin, and ceiling ; and she filled
The corridors with monks, some highly skilled
In cookery, or garden lore, or dreams
That peer beyond the sun's far-reaching beams,
And bear the soul to Heaven ; and she would dress
The abbey garden, now a wilderness,

With thoughts of flowers—the fairies hid between,
Lending enchantment to the lovely scene,—
In fact the fancied Abbey looked more fair
Than when it flowered its Spring in the rude air
Of long ago, when all the world was rent
With zeal to build that hateful monument
Of slaughtered bodies to the name of Christ,—
As though *His* love could ever be enticed
To dwell with man in such brutality :
She glossed this o'er with old-world pageantry,
For in her tender heart she could not paint
A cruel hero as she would a saint,—
So when that mood came on she banished quick
Those visionary walls of Walberswick.

These lovely dreams came best to her at night
When her thoughts melted in the moon's soft light
And all the world was bathed in velvet hues
And leaves were freshened with the tenderest dews
Sprinkled by fairies o'er the parchèd earth,
That poetry might blossom into birth ;
At such times her romantic nature blazed
In 'wildering ecstasy ; her eyes all dazed
Saw visions greater than the mind can form
When grappling with Death amid the storm
Of furious passion 'twixt the wind and sea,
Struggling with stupid strength for mastery.

And so it chanced that 'neath a brooding moon,
On a soft evening in voluptuous June,
She met a youth who from his toils had strayed
Out of hard London, where his health had paid
The usual sacrifice to ill-spent hours
Of dissipation in fair ladies' bowers ;—
The country luring him with dreams of health
And golden sunshine full of hidden wealth ;—
And as he slid into her vision bright,
She hailed him as a veritable Knight
Pale in the moonbeams ; yet she spoke no word,
But fluttered quickly like a frightened bird
Behind a buttress, hiding from his gaze
While still observing all his well-bred ways.
At first she noticed his soft, languid air,
His easy graceful motion,—all too rare
Amongst the country youth she knew by heart,—
And then she wondered what could be his part
In Nature, as he lounged at close of day
Lazily smoking his young life away ;
What could he trouble his young soul about
Watching the wreaths of smoke die slowly out
Into the moon ?   The beauty of the scene,
The softened outlines and the magic green,
The holy halo round the silver orb,
Seemed not his wondering Fancy to absorb ;
His thoughts were far away ; each whiff of smoke

Rose like an incense to the dreams that broke
Upon his vision ; once her Fancy thought
Each poisoned whiff his poisoned mind upbrought,
Just as the smoke blown from the mountain-spires
Reveals th' existence of earth's hidden fires ;
But for this thought she chid her Fancy sore
And then began to hallow him the more ;
Telling her Fancy that the fires of Earth
Coin diamonds and gems of priceless worth,
And gold and silver and all precious stones,
Behind which women ofttimes hide their groans ;
And so, she thought, his fire of mind now wrought
Fine interlacing arabesques of thought
And dreams of goodness, suiting well her mind
Which to the evils of the world was blind ;
It would have tortured her to hide a sting
Within the words her gentle mind would string
Like pearls together, when with simple ease
She talked with worldly women,—born to tease
The gentle heart of Truth by acting lies ;
Deeming their conduct elegant and wise.

Chained to her buttress Lilian felt at length
That Time was fleeing with impetuous strength
Away from her and she must homeward fly ;
But she was much too modest to defy
The silent stranger, so she made essay

To seek an exit by some other way
From her charmed ruin, and tore her dainty dress
In breaking through a bramble-wilderness.
But it were better to destroy a gown
Than humble country pride to London town.

HAROLD'S LIFE BEFORE MEETING LILIAN.

He therefore smoked unconscious of her eyes,
And never dreamed that such a lovely prize
Was near to him. He had hard thoughts to think ;
For he had driven his soul too near the brink
Of ruin ; yet was he still a-tune with joy ;
For he was but a rosebud of a boy
Opening the leaves of manhood, and he knew
How all the world admired the good and true
And only thought their own heart's wickedness
Was worthy cultivation or excuse,
As weeds, forsooth, may lovely flowers produce
In skilful hands. He who the world doth shock
Bruises his head against unfeeling rock
And dies unmourned. He therefore knew the fate
That he would suffer if he raised the hate
Of the hard, calculating, sensual world,
Who 'gainst the glass of conscience fiercely hurled
Their hard hypocrisy, and lived, and lied,
And cheated till all tenderness had died.

Methinks a gentle heart would rather paint
A noble sinner than a narrow saint,
A sweet, though erring soul, than a mere toy
Made out of wooden creeds ; and so this boy
Bruising his budding life, was sweeter far
Than his hard father, distant as a star
From warm humanity, with heart congealed
In frigid zones of thought, although he kneeled
In daily worship to the Central Heart
Of glowing life, thinking God would impart
Through Love's warm arteries Eternal Rest.
Yet what he really wanted in his breast
Was an Eternal Unrest and a glow
Of sympathetic love for all below.
Love could not bless a father who had spurned
His erring son from home and never yearned
To take him to his heart again.   Oh ! Love !
Why dost thou never rend the Heavens above
And show thy beauty to these selfish minds
Whose sight is covered with Night's darkest blinds
Of ignorance ?   If men would but unlearn
Their selfishness, then would they Love discern !
So Harold having lost his mother's life
While he was fretting though his baby-strife
Knew not the pity of a parent's eye,
And left his home with half-regretful sigh
Ere he had blushed away his tender teens

Amid his dearly loved ancestral scenes :—
The park, the manor-house, the lodge, the gate,
The hundred glories of a squire's estate.

Banished ! and for a mocking word, a jest
At his strange father's superstitious quest
For his own soul's salvation : "Open wide
Your pockets and your bounteous arms," he cried,
"Be kind and good to all as Christ was kind,
And then you may feel something of His mind ;
But to believe that selfish life, and prayers,
And strange, unfeeling, hypocritic airs,
Will save your neck upon the Judgment Day,
Is to be like a beggar by the way,
Expecting luxuries and influence great
Poured in his lazy lap as he doth wait.
As if a great, good God could grant a life eternal
To souls who love to breathe an atmosphere in-
      fernal."
These words to his hard father cut like knives
Into his conscience, and as one who rives
A tree asunder, so he fiercely tore
His heart's affections to the very core ;
And Harold, unprotected, sought new life
And found it in a busy London strife,
And who can wonder that his heart was turned
Against religion as so ill-discerned

By half the world, who never yearn to bless
With flowers of Love this weed-strewn wilderness.

But Harold months before had felt the spell
Of a fair maiden's love, and who shall tell
The flutterings of her heart when he revealed
The news of banishment, but half concealed
By his sad face : like a wild rose distressed
With weeping rain her head she drooped and pressed
Against his bosom in a flood of tears,
And nothing would relieve her trembling fears
But promises of his companionship
Extracted charily from his still lip ;
And so the morrow-morn to her rose gay,
For she was his companion on the way
To London City, caring not a whit
What all the wondering world might think of it,
But quite content to be a whispered tale
Of woe amongst the dwellers in her vale,
Than a lone maiden, drooping, all forlorn
Amid the aspirations of the corn
Ripening to Truth beneath the inspiring sun ;
For to her little heart there was but one
Adornment, one delight, one truth to see,—
The light that shone from his eyes' constancy.
Forgive her, sisters, for she was a child,
A country rose-bud easily beguiled

By Love's warm sun to blossom all too soon,
Mistaking Spring-time for the month of June.
Her parents were retainers of the Squire
And knew their rose-bud in that scorching fire
Would droop and die ; and they together wept,
But no warm comfort to their dulled hearts crept.

The old Squire cared not for their sorrow smart
But cursed their Mary's silly little heart
And doubly cursed his son, his blighted joy,
Calling on Ruin to destroy his boy,
And with these curses on his bitter tongue
He bowed the knees in church, and prayed and
    sung.
(His dead wife's spirit in a dream that night
Wrapped up her earthly form and tried to fright
His stony, arid heart without avail,—
The Devil had more feeling in his tail.)

Now Harold lived with Mary quite retired
And he for months was constant and admired
Her wild-rose blushes ; but there came a day
When cultured rose-buds stole his heart away,
And Mammon placed before him riches rare,
And his pure moral nature in despair
Fled from him frightened out by luxury,
Soft self-indulgence, sensuality,

And all the wild temptations riches fling
Around the simple hearted ; these would bring
His soul to desolation.   One nymph came
And burnt his being as with fiery flame,
Tortured him, tempted   him, and   wrecked   his
        peace,
And bound him to her for the broken lease
Of his young life.   A scheming woman she,
A bitter scorner of humanity,
With winning, graceful manners, and soft eyes
That ne'er betrayed a moment of surprise ;
A serpent subtly dressed ; a lady born ;
Too wise to show the world her cruel scorn ;
And with her lily arms she fondled him,
And made him pander to her every whim,
And when he left her laughed at her deceit,
Yet kept him slave beneath her pretty feet.
Oh ! what a picture art thou, Lady Grace,
Of how society can mould a face,
To hide the feelings of the heart within,
Veiled by a delicate and painted skin !
And thou, poor Mary, by the country bred,
Wilt thou, wild rose-bud, raise thy drooping head,
Or die amongst dead daffodils of Spring,
A lovely flower, soiled, and sorrowing ?

THEIR FIRST LIFE TOGETHER.

Alas ! for him who hath 'mid bricks been reared,
Inhaling oxygen all soot besmeared,
And never hath a country valley trod,
For he who studies Nature studies God,
And in her opened palm may clearly read
Life's trembling history.   We hardly need
The sacred Bible or man's written word,
For God in Nature may be plainly heard.
And Harold as he sat beneath the moon
On that soft evening in voluptuous June,
Heard some one preaching to him from the skies,
And through that teaching, eloquent and wise,
His trouble vanished and he slowly felt
The heart of Nature in his being melt.
That heart he knew could sob in tears of rain,
And then in sunshine brightly smile again,
He knew, too, how the twinkling stars of heaven
Laughed at his prattle when a child of seven.
And now he felt the moon re-silver o'er
His mirror conscience, Nature would restore.
Home then he went soothed by her gentle hand
And slept as calm as any in the land.
While Lilian on her bed—a blush-rose spray
Tossed in the breeze of Love—all restless lay.

'Twixt midnight and the morn her soul had grown
Too large for its environments : alone
With Nature's hopes and mystic shadowings
Of life Beyond, her soul had taken wings
And felt ofttimes unutterable things.
But now she felt a higher influence reign,
For Love had nestled in her dreaming brain,
Growing forthwith prolific of sweet thought ;
Yet p'raps her florid Fancy had o'erwrought
The charm of Harold 'neath the silvery rays
Of the pale moon ; (and naught can charm the gaze
Like that loved orb ;) What if the charm should
    flee
When she might hear his lip's philosophy
Or listen to the cadence of his voice
And find it passionless ? could Love rejoice
In harsh and strident tones ?   Must it not die
In discord ?   And so with many a sigh
At these brain-trumpetings of Night alarms
She sought with morning light her mother's arms :
One kiss dispersed her fears which soon distilled
Their fretful spirits into tears that filled
Her lovely eyes, like dew-drops in a flower,
Born in the passion of Night's silent hour.

Ere breakfast came she to the garden stole
And with the blushing peaches sunned her soul ;

Then from the clear-eyed water in the brook
Sweet watercresses in her hands she took
And brought them in with roses red and white
Which Nature beautified for her delight ;
And while her pet-thrush sang his tenderest tune
Fresh dainties from the ripening hand of June
She deftly gathered ; red tomatoes stored
With sleeping sunbeams, and a magic gourd
Full of cool juices syphoned from the earth,—
A mystery to Lilian from its birth ;
And then the raspberries and strawberries too
She gathered fast and to the dairy flew
To skim the cream that she might with the maid
Have the white damask delicately laid
In time to greet her father's loving eyes,
And hear his morning comments good and wise :
But on this morning in a mute despair—
Love laughing through her beauty-dreaming
    hair,—
With thoughts sigh-spoken and a drooping head
She lived on Love and left her daily bread.

But ere the full-bloom of the morn had past
She wandered to the beach and saw at last
Her Unknown with a child at play ; their glee
As sportive as a minuet at sea
Between the dancing waves when wind and sun

Whistle and laugh at all their bounding fun ;
This sight aroused a whirling, sensuous crowd
Of feelings, and her heart beat quick and loud,
And then the problem came,—how could she
　　speak
Or look at him ?　A maiden should be meek
And modest, not o'er-bold ; but we have all
To answer to the ever-varying call
Of circumstance ; and therefore that sweet child
Went romping backwards laughing shrill and wild,
Then tripped and fell upon the yielding sand
Just as a wave was making for the land ;
Fair, anxious Lilian rushed forth to save,
And got herself entangled in the wave ;
Then Harold, hat in hand, politely came
And said he feared that he was much to blame,
And brushed her down, while she consoled the
　　boy
Who brought to her this unexpected joy.
And when she found the little child was drenched
And shivering with tiny fingers clenched,
She begged that she might take the darling home
If Harold would consent with them to come.
And he well knowing Walberswick too far,
Consented to escort this maiden star
 To her sweet Southwold home, and as he went
He felt a radiance from her heart was sent

Into his own, as though an influence reigns
That binds us heart to heart in silken chains.

She spun a web about him artlessly
From which he never more himself could free,
And prattled lightly, as they walked along,
Of tennis tourneys and the last new song
From all-absorbing London ; of the views
Around the coast ; and all the local news ;
But ne'er before had his rapt ear heard sound
More dulcet, words more true, or more profound :
So easy 'tis for Love to magnify
Its sweet adorings, and with pride espy
Beauties too modest for the light above :
No study doth absorb the heart like Love.
To him frail Mary was no more Love's shrine ;
Her eyes might weep and all her spirit pine
And waste away, but he no more could find
The silken cord that should their spirits bind ;
'Twas snapped for ever ; and dear Lady Grace
Could never more use her deceitful face
To lure him to her, for her day had gone,
And in his heart he heard the knell forlorn
Of all his life in London ; he would sweep
As in a hidden garden-rubbish heap
The dead affections of those days ; the flowers
Tossed to him in those sweet, wild, wanton hours ;

But could he thus obliterate the past ?
Has it not life and feeling to the last ?

Meanwhile fair Lilian careful of the child,
Most tenderly its little heart beguiled
With thoughts of soft, warm beds and dancing fires,
And prospects of most picturesque attires,
While his damp clothes before the fire she dried ;
And so he trotted laughing by her side
Full of sweet confidence and lisping truth
More puzzling to manhood than to youth.

And when they to her love-lit garden came,
The sunflowers stared at them with eyes aflame ;
While modest roses blushed in mute surprise
And turned their heads from wondering at the
    skies ;
And beds of pansies dyed with purple stains
And yellow splashes, felt the magic pains
Of brooding Love ; (no more " heart's-ease " for
    them
Until a purple-sorrow-diadem
They formed above her grave ;) and lilies pure
From far Japan, felt they could not endure
The pangs of life with Lilian's heart elsewhere,
And drooped their wax-like heads in dumb de-
    spair ;

But Lilian laughed to see their jealous ways
On this glad morning of this day of days,
And said as Harold through the gateway went :—
" I fancy my loved flowers would fain resent
Your presence in their midst ; they look so sad
Instead of laughing at us bright and glad."
And Harold promptly said with smiling air :—
" I envy them the constant loving care
Of the most beautiful of all the fair,
And if I stir their calm felicity
There may be grounds for their sad jealousy."
And Lilian blushing, as a maiden should,
Said tenderly :—" I would not, if I could,
Alter the course of this most happy morn,
And yet I well deserve the quiet scorn
Of all my darling flowers who are half-slain
By the long absence of refreshing rain,
And begged me so to water them this day ;—
But someone drove my thought of them away."
Then with the little boy she fled inside
And told her mother of th' inrushing tide,
And while she put him in her own pure bed
A spirit-light on her fair face was shed,
Like to the magic sheen a sunbeam weaves
When glancing lovingly on young green leaves.
Her mother wondered at the rapturous look
Until she heard the part that Harold took

In th'adventure, and watched her daughter's breast
Heave with some strange excitement unconfessed,
And heard that Harold's name she did but know
" Five happy golden minutes past " and how
He waited in the garden by her flowers,
" Counting the minutes p'raps as lovelorn hours."

How could she this fine language understand?
So Lilian took her gently by the hand
(Kissing the boy) to show her Harold's face,
Hopeful that such a lovely sight might chase
The doubtings from her eyes : to her the sight
Would drive away the blackness of the Night
And bring the Sun, but would her mother be
Inclined to view her heart's philosophy
With favouring eyes ? how full she was of fears,
For wisdom only comes with ripened years,
But when she saw her mother's kind eyes melt
As Harold's interlacing hand she felt,
Her heart beat wondrous life ; of course she knew
That words of mother-wisdom would ensue ;
And soon she heard :— " Love that comes quick
          like yours,
" A summer fancy ofttimes quickly cures ;
" Be not too hasty, Lilian."   But he stayed
To lunch, he clung about their hearts and paid
Sweet court to Lilian ; and when he left

Her mother told him they would be bereft
Of pleasure if he came no more ; and he,
Full of his own warm heart's necessity,
Promised to call upon them every day
Until his holidays should flee away.

———

Part II. The Courtship.

Love is the alphabet of the Heavenly tongue,
The passion of the soul by poets sung,
The measure of the heart of all mankind,
Yet measureless itself, for none can find
Its height, or depth, or fulness of desire ;
(It lives for ever with the heart on fire,)
And none can bind it, though a slave it lives
Subservient to the very life it gives.

And day by day these truths in Harold's heart
Were dropped like choicest seeds that fain would
    start
To beauteous life ; yet sadness marked his face
As in his complex nature he could trace
Closely embedded round those budding seeds
The living roots of the obnoxious weeds
Sown in the days gone by.   Oh ! for some charm

To make him pure ; to cleanse and calm
His now regretful heart !   Can no one change
A fungus growth into a lily ?   Strange
No chemist great has yet found out a way
To stop the moral nature from decay !
Better be pure within, though foul without,
Than have an angel put your soul to rout
By dazzling purity into your eyes,—
Delusive beacons smiling pretty lies.—
Eyes may be clear and soft, skin lily-white,
Only to hide corruption from the sight.

But Love was strong and Love was paramount,
And Love would burn corruption in its fount
Of fire, and from the embers bid uprise
A hallowed spirit soaring to the skies.
And Love was kind and Love was beautiful,
And he was young and would be dutiful
To high-born Love, that alchemist of hearts,
Transforming brutes to gods by magic arts ;
Love was the world-known chemist who could stay
His moral fall and with him soar away
Into diviner airs.   Away with grief !
For Love would bring his conscience sweet relief,
And all the past would shroud itself in mist,
Now that warm Love his very lips had kissed.

What were those past sweet moments ? Love ?
    or Death
With all the simulated fevered breath
Of Love ?   Or hot wild passion of the flesh
Shaken to madness in the silken mesh
Of changeful Fancy ?   What if Lilian heard
Him question why she was o'er all preferred ?
What if she looked at him with her pure eyes
And read his thoughts ?   Would she not then
    despise
His subtleties ?   Love *was not* in the past,—
That ghost at which his spirit stood aghast
In frenzied fear !   Could no one kill a ghost ?
Needs it more courage to destroy a host
Of living heads than one pale ghostly thought
Which ever rises in the mind o'erwrought ?
Oh ! for some sponge to wipe away the past,
And Joshua's power to hold the present fast,
By bidding that warm sun of Love stand still
Upon that gently sloping Southwold hill !

So Harold brooded o'er his love, new-born
Amid the roses and the whispering corn
Of sleepy Southwold : lovely were the days ;
Light-hearted Summer sang her tenderest lays
With flower-scented breaths, while she entranced
The land with an encircling smile that glanced

On all alike, and made the happy earth
Smile back again in wild contagious mirth.
And she would beat her magic music wand,
And call her choir together near the trees,
(For every insect was of Summer fond
And ever sought her listening ear to please.)
She made a bee drone forth a solo sweet
While searching honied clover at her feet,
And taught the thrush to pipe his hautboy
    tones
Above the buzzing bee's soft tonic drones ;
And bade the prima-donna of the skies
Trill a song heavenward in a spiral rise
Piercing the outer blue of Paradise
To show the way ; and as it upward went
The breeze would blow a soft accompaniment
In Harold's ear, (not with the heavy hand
Of some musicians' loud orchestral band,
Which would have frightened from the sky-lark
    free
All thoughts of Heaven's magic minstrelsy.
But) murmuring busy music all around
The sky-lark carolled to th' enchanting sound.
(He must be Nature's child whoe'er attains
A magic influence o'er his brothers' brains,
And must to Beauty bow a reverent knee,
Ere he may join the Muses' company.)

And Harold learnt from Lilian how to feel
The rapture of the sky-lark's wild appeal
To listening Heaven.   He never knew before
The wistful beauties of Earth's flower-strewn floor,
But now he saw a thousand lovely eyes
Peep through Earth's carpet at the watchful skies ;
And sometimes on the grass he feared to tread,
(Such softness in his heart had Lilian shed,)
Lest he might trample on some form divine
That Lilian worshipped as a fairy's shrine.
Lilian was his law ; the waves roared forth
Her name ; the Earth spoke Lilian ; and the North,
Led on by Boreas, blew loud and clear,
" Lilian ! Lilian ! " in his rapt lover's ear ;
And the warm South with softly lingering breath
Whispered her name, then died a placid death ;
There was no other name writ in the sky,
As all the stars of Heaven went floating by
Upon the wings of Night, but her fond name ;
The sun revealed it, too, in passion-flame !

Each day his heart would seek her and would find
New beauties in her cultivated mind,
New dreams of goodness, new devotion given
To some deserving creature under heaven.
A Spirit-revelation pure and fresh,
With an eternal mission to all flesh

Was Lilian : just as a flower may be
Proof of the presence of the Deity
To reverent eyes.   Who can behold a face
Of beaming goodness and refuse to trace
The great Divinity that lives and breathes
In all the forms He to grim Death bequeaths ?
Death only gets from God the dross he craves,—
Mean miser gloating o'er our human graves,—
While like a flash of light we soar away
Into the regions of diviner day !
Oh ! for more hearts like Lilian's ! which could
    move
E'en sensual Harold from his earth-bound groove ;
He, like an Ethiope, pining to be white,
Basked in the pureness of her mind of light.

        Spirit of Maidenhood !
          Dazzlingly pure,
      Bright as the diamond
          Made to endure,
        Shed thy light ever
          On rich and on poor.

        Let none deceive thee
          With bright, pretty toys,
      And tempt thee to barter
          Thine innocent joys

For secret emotion
  That slaves and annoys.

Be like the sunbeam
  That sheds on the street
A light-hearted gaiety
  Buoying the feet
Of those who work ever
  In cold and in heat.

Be like the mountain
  Touching the skies,
Firm and enduring,
  Proof 'gainst surprise,
Looking for ever
  To catch the sunrise.

And if it come not,
  Be like the snow,
Pure in the altitudes
  Heat cannot glow,
Better be that
  Than a rivulet low,

Flooding the valleys
  Where men come and go,
Ready to poison

The pure overflow
With the vile refuse
Their mammon-mills know.

But if the Sun-Love
Rise on thy soul,
Circle around it
As the days roll,
Till it absorb thee
In its great whole.

A fortnight's dalliance with each other's heart
Made each one conscious that they ne'er could
part
Without tempestuous floods of swelling grief.
(Cupid is ever an inveterate thief,
And steals us all, unconscious of ourselves ;
Could we but place our feelings on our shelves
In iron safes and take the key away,
Cupid would circumvent us every day.)
And Harold's lips grew bold with tender words,
And love-sick cooings like an amorous bird's,
Until at last they sought a lingering kiss
Upon the lips of Lilian. Oh ! what bliss
Came then to both their hearts ! 'twas on a night
When moonbeams kissed the waves with fond
delight

As they beneath them danced with liquid feet
Dissolving in each other ; ne'er so sweet
A motion could be e'er conceived or seen
(Tho' nymphs might dance their lightest on the
    green).
And what could Harold and fair Lilian do
But melt in one another's being too ?

Then Harold said to Lilian : " Yon star-pearl
Dropping its silver tears upon the sky
They call fair Venus, but my English girl
Is lovelier far than that frail memory
Of ancient days, when fertile Homer sung
To Grecian ears, and still keeps ever young.
Her heart is shrouded in the misty past,
But here I hold a human flower so fast,
With love so dear, that I would sooner feel
Her melt away within my burning grasp
Than have another hated rival steal
Her sainted image from my jealous clasp :
Tell me, sweet Lilian, that it ne'er can be."
And he upon her lips stamped kisses three
As solemn pledges of fidelity.
And she had only simple words to say :—
" Harold, you know that I shall love alway,"
And sealed them with three kisses as her bond,
  Unneeded pledges from a heart so fond.

Blind Night saw not her blushes, but her love
Awoke sweet music in the harps above,
And thrilled through all her being into song :

LILIAN'S SONG.

The crocus like a warrior bold
　　With spear defies the clay,
Then forms a loving cup to hold
　　Spring's store of sunbeams gay,
And having wrought its fancy old,
　　Contented,—dies away.
Blaze out, warm sun of Love, and dress
Each flower with dainty loveliness.

Bare rose-trees in the Winter seem
　　Unconscious, drear, and dead,
But in the Spring begin to dream
　　In pink, and white, and red,
And having kissed the sun's warm beam,
　　In Autumn's arms fall dead.
Blaze out, warm sun of Love, and give
Sweet rose-buds to me while I live.

And I like some loved flower of earth
　　My summer-passion feel,
I am exalted past my worth,

No rose can be more real,
Yet, Love, thou art a spirit-birth
No frost can e'er congeal.
Blaze out, warm sun of Love, and light
A maiden in her passion-flight ;

Waft me away, Love, with gauzy wings dressed,
Into the dream of the rose-coloured West,
Into the heart of Thy spirit at rest.

And Harold listened with a tender fear,
As her pure spirit-breath entranced his ear,
The air seemed far too sacred for his soul,
Filled with weird music like a death-bell's toll.
How could he look upon a mind so pure
And not be dazzle-blinded more and more,
Just as the eye gets sightless in the sun.
Yon staring star gazed like a cold-eyed nun
Upon him, and rebuked him for his pride ;
But the warm breath of Lilian as she sighed
Her last sweet note to Heaven, rose like a cloud,
And blurred the picture of the star so proud,
And·he was man again, frail, mortal man,
As through his being sensual rapture ran ;
The cloud went past the star to melt in Heaven,
While he fermented in a fleshly leaven.
This storm of earth-bred passion 'mid the flash

Of spirit lightning made a constant clash
Of feelings in his soul.   He would be high
And touch the heavens with Lilian, but the cry
Of low emotion often drowned the speech
Of his aspiring nature.   Ye who teach
The yearning hearts of children, know the pain
Through which they struggle to a higher plane.
Kiss after kiss on Lilian fell, until
She tore herself from his magnetic will
Flustered with strange confusion ; then he felt
His sensual nature into spirit melt,
And he was man again, but pure, redeemed,
Full of the glory of which saints have dreamed.
And then he sang :—

HAROLD'S SONG.

The sky is dark, my Love, and we
Have watched the moon dip silently
Her silver bosom in the sea.

There will she lave earth's taint away,
And cleanse her dress of silver gray,
Hiding herself behind the Day.

Oh ! sea, I fain would wash my soul
In thy pure waves, and onward roll
To ice-cold airs around the pole.

There should my soul a prism be,
And Love's warm sun would shine thro' me
In rainbow tints of purity.

And on an iceberg I would sail
To tell my Lilian all the tale
Of my poor heart so weak and frail.

Then could she in her bosom wear
My soul, all purified and fair,—
An amulet of Love most rare.

And Lilian loved the song
And stored it in her mem'ry 'mid the throng
Of lyrics that had lulled her heart to rest
When tossed amid the turmoils of her breast ;
But this song crowned them all ; 'twas Harold's
     soul
Laid bare to her, aspiring to the goal
Of perfect life.   How she would love him now
And deck with garlands his poetic brow !
So in the moonlight Harold led her home
Filled with the breezes wafted o'er the foam
Of dazzling waters ; and he pressed her lips
To his, and 'twixt the dainty honey sips
Declared, that ere the summer should have passed,
They would be joined in happy wedlock fast.

And ere the night had wooed them to their beds
They both knelt suppliant to the silver heads
Of Lilian's parents dear, to whom they talked
Through midnight of their plans, till in there
    stalked
The ghost of sleep with sensuous, drowsy eyes,
And bade them rest until the new sunrise.

SPIRIT FOREBODINGS.

Say you the sun will reluctantly rise, and moodily
        sink in the West,
            Cladding the day
            In a suit of gray,
        And thus unbecomingly drest
Will sulk from my bride on her wedding morn
As though it were better she had not been born ?

Say you the birds will not sing in the trees, that
        the heart of the world will stand still,
            And beat never more,
            In Humanity's core,
        Because I have bent to Love's will,
And placidly buried my loved one with me
'Neath the sobs of the lips of Life's surface-torn
    sea ?

Nay ! the sun will leap dancing o'er mountains of
   Hope, to the pipe of the passionate lark,
    As upwards he springs
    On melody's wings,
  In his joy at the flight of the dark ;
The face of fair nature will smile on her bliss
And hurry, light-hearted, her blushes to kiss ;

And the heart of Humanity then will beat fast and
   throb through the delicate veins,
    And passion and glow,
    In heat or in snow,
  With the thrills of Life's pleasures and pains,
And ever triumphant, with sympathy great,
It will beat with the stars at Heaven's gateway,—
  and wait.

On that new morn the village heard the news
And plans were laid to honour and amuse
The plighted pair ; and now 'tis often told
How Southwold, decked with bunting bright and
  bold,
Made holiday upon that wedding fair,
And filled with merriment the summer air.
But 'tis remembered, too, how on that eve
The sun seemed loath his golden bed to leave,
As in the west he lay in dreams of rest,
Until a spasm passed o'er Earth's full breast,

And clouds rose black and angry in the East,
Like to the shape of a devouring beast,
The wind shrieked hissing at some unseen prey,
And all the heavens were quickly draped in gray
And hid the golden sun ; then lightning came
And wrote upon the clouds its vivid name
In zigzag signs ; then came the thunder crash
Almost as quickly as the lightning flash
That fell upon the steeple like the fire
Of God ; tore out the stone-work ; crushed the
    spire ;
Hurled down the flagstaff splintered like a reed ;
Then hail was scattered like the poppy seed
Upon the ground ; then fled the storm away,
And in the burnished West all peaceful lay
The drowsy sun. " A portent ! " muttered some,
" The finger of the Lord ! " " A time will come
Of sorrow for the pair ! " some gossips said,
Shaking in fear each superstitious head.
While he and Lilian left the storm behind
Tearing to London, winnowing the wind
In the swift train, to the mystic life,
The " Open Sesame " of man and wife.

Part III.   The Wedded Life.

WHO can be quiet in this world of storm ?
Our dreams of peace evanish ere they form
In our quick minds, just as the snow-flakes change
In the hot palm of Summer, into strange,
Cold, silent tears ; nothing can be at rest,
Not e'en the baby dreaming at the breast ;
E'en the hard Earth will quiver at our feet
Torn by the energies of cold and heat.
The feeling that our young emotion charms
Re-lives in opportunity's ripe arms,
And, therefore, many a spirit grows deformed
When by the tempests of the world be-stormed ;
Watch how the trees bend inward from the sea
Blown by the sea-swept winds incessantly,
And how the flowers that laugh up at the sun
When brimming o'er with warm Midsummer fun,
Will hang their pretty heads before King Frost,
Death-stricken, nipped, with all their colours lost.
Behold that valley sleeping in the sun,
Cooled by pure rivulets that onward run,
Fretting towards the sea ! no sound is heard
Save lazy breaths of wind or pipe of bird,
And yet we know that all the peaceful scene

Beneath its variegated coat of green,
Trembles with all the heat of struggling life
Aiming at high perfection in its strife.
So as we breathe our sensuous life away,
The elements on our fine spirits play
As on a harp ; and to the Heavens we sing
A thrilling song of joy, or, sighing, wring
A dirge of sorrow from heart-strings of woe.
The music of our souls doth ebb and flow
Like the wild sea ; but to divine the song,
Is given to few amongst the listening throng
Who strive from wakeful Morn to brooding Night,
To catch the spirit of Man's song aright.

But surely Harold now had found true rest
Upon his lovely Lilian's snowy breast !
And all the world might storm in useless rage
While those two love-birds in their marriage cage
Flirted with serious Time !   Their bill and coo
Went on unmindful of the wind that blew
Around the aching world.   Nations might fall,
But they were to each other all in all,—
A deep romance of Love ! What force could break
The bond that bound them ?   Not the mighty
        quake
Of the hard-crusted Earth ! not poverty !
Nor pain ! nor yet the ghastly tragedy

Of body-snatching Death ! For now he felt
As though his heart might into Lilian's melt
As in a crucible, to be recast
In the most perfect form of Love at last
That she—his heart's refiner—could desire !
He fain would burn his dross in Love's pure fire.

They lived in London now ; his business brought
Throughout the day a troubled sea of thought,
But in the evening with his lovely wife
The choicest ecstasy we wring from life
Was his ; she was so happy in her pride,
As he sat beaming on her by her side,
Molten with love. They talked of Southwold
    sights
And culled anew the flowery delights
They had together in that wooing time,
When Summer had forgot the Winter rime.

But Harold, like some fine-strung instrument
On which all passions play, at length was rent
With a desire for change ; the key had grown
Monotonous, and in some other tone
The melody of Love would sound more dear,
And be more pleasing to his Lilian's ear.
He chid himself for keeping her so long
Away from gay Society's gathering throng ;

She must be dull indeed !   But she aloud
Protested that no sort of cultured crowd
Would ever charm her like the hours of bliss
They spent alone with Love's most sacred kiss.

But he felt sure their life was not a dream
Of mighty aspirations 'mid the gleam
Of an imagined Heaven.   He fain would get
A higher peak of aspiration yet,
And so he took his Lilian to the halls
Of all his friends ; to concerts, and to balls ;
And he grew prouder of her still, for none
Looked lovelier than his own sweet Lilian
Amid the crowd of fashion, where she drew
Obsequious courtiers her fair face to view,
Who made bright quips with her and pretty jests,
Till she was envied by the lady-guests.
But Harold ne'er felt jealous,—only proud
To see his wife admired of all the crowd.

One night at some high function Harold met
The dainty priestess of the " inner-set,"
His old enchantress, tempting Lady Grace,
Who bade him take her " to the lovely face
Of charming Lilian, that she might adore
Where other worshippers had knelt before."
He said : " Not so : pray let her live apart

From all the elements that wrecked my heart
Upon the rocks of thoughtless gaiety ;
Be kind to her, my friend, and pity me."
" Nay, nay ; you silly boy, I am no fool,
You would not have me sent again to school,
The world will only whisper wicked tales,
If you keep Lilian amongst the males ;
Besides, as we have now been seen to meet,
It is but natural that I should greet
Your pretty wife, or all the world will say
Our friendship will not bear the light of day."
So Harold most reluctantly was driven
To introduce a serpent to his heaven.

Ah ! Harold, can you really hide the past ?
Has it not life and feeling to the last ?
Will not the early culture we receive,
Haunt us from sun-gilt Morn to shadowy Eve ?
And were you not delighted once again
To be by Lady Grace's wit re-slain ?

Too true, alas ! and Lilian felt as well
Th' enchanting influence of the Lady's spell ;
No moonlight magic poured thro' leafy trees
With dried leaves rustling in the mystic breeze,
Was needed to complete her wiles at night :
She wrought them in the ball-room's blazing light

Observed by all ; and all could watch her will
Slowly but surely all resistance still.
Society adored dear Lady Grace,
For she was daughter of a noble race
Whose high progenitors had writ their name
Large in the annals of her country's fame ;
And she had mighty patronage and wealth,
And, best of gifts,—exuberance of health,
And her great beauty was a sight to see,
Entrancing as a rose's mystery ;
But she was subtly wicked, gaily bad,
And not a breath of scandal made her sad.

Thus pure-eyed Lilian met subtle Grace,
Who showed no blush of shame upon her face,
But talked so tenderly of Life and Death,
And showed such sympathy with human breath,
That Lilian was transported in her praise,
And next day quoted Harold many a phrase,
Born on her fertile lips, as treasured words
More hopeful than the singing of the birds.
But Harold never told his Lilian dear,
That Lady Grace had whispered in his ear
At some chance meeting, later, on that night,
" How deftly she had wooed his lady bright,
With words of wisdom that her eyes had read
And stored as nonsense in her flighty head

Some years ago ; ne'er dreaming she would be
A lady-teacher of philosophy ! "
Nor did he tell her how he laughed with glee
At all this whispered impropriety.

That laugh was fatal : sudden as it came
It shed upon his cheeks a rosy shame,
And e'en the generous fumes of ruby wine
Rising like incense in its human shrine,
Could not endow it with one single charm ;
He therefore sought his Lilian in alarm,
And found her drooping like a lily pale
Swept by the fury of a western gale :—
" Is aught the matter, Lilian ? " he said,
As playfully he touched her pretty head,
And heard reply : " Darling, I am unwell !
But why my nerves are wracked I cannot tell,
I feel as though some influence had passed
Throughout my system like a chilly blast ;
It can be only fancy : let us go."
Yet all the way she talked with rapid flow
Of Lady Grace's charming gifts and power,
Until she slept at last in her Love-bower,
And dreamed this dream :—

LILIAN'S DREAM.
The moon looked o'er the shoulder of a hill,

With many a tender, sweet, magnetic thrill,
Into a valley's heart ; which in amaze
Oped all its beauties to her love-lorn gaze.
The woods seemed loath to sleep while they were
    kissed
By her soft glances, but the treacherous mist
Lay drowsily embracing the warm earth,
Unmindful of her gaze ; 'twas surely worth
A golden argosy to be so wooed
By such bewitching looks ; sweet Love might
    brood
With the entrancéd woods eternally,
(And never pine again for what may be)
In such a scene : a Paradise more fair
Than moonlight streaming through the dark blue
    air
Upon melodious waterfalls, whose songs
Will lull away a host of fancied wrongs,
Is scarce conceivable.   Lilian loved the sight,
And wandered, pensive, far into the night,
Amid the ever-changing lights and shades
Wrought by the moon amid the dark green
    glades,
Until she came to where a wild rose-tree
Trailed its blush-blossoms in a canopy
Over a mossy, old, romantic well,
In which she peered to read its magic spell,

And, awe-struck, saw a snake of glittering green,
Whose diamond eyes lit up the mossy scene,
Writhing amid the ever-moving sand,
And seeming every moment to expand,
Until at length it lost its serpent shape,
And turned itself into a grinning ape,
Who with a scream tore all its skin away,
And then revealed a lady young and gay.
With wonder Lilian looked upon the face,
And found it imaged charming Lady Grace,
Who said no word to her, but looked most proud,
And then evanished in a silver cloud
Which fled along the mountain to the moon.
At this fair Lilian felt inclined to swoon,
But that she saw her husband's form arise
White, like a ghost, with anger in his eyes,
He looked at Lilian with a fierce disdain,
Then glided silently along the plain,
Climbed the drear mountain full of shadows deep,
And then ascended up the moonbeams steep,
Into the moon itself where Grace had flown.
" Fled   in   the   moonbeams !   whither   art   thou
        gone,
Thou soul of glory ? " Lilian cried, distressed,
" Wilt thou not soon return and make me blest,
Or speak to me once more in some fine way,
Knowing I worship all thou hast to say ?

String all the stars together into 'words,
And make a wonder for the vulgar herds
To newspaper about.   Let not Night roll
Until thou write thy thoughts on heaven's blue
    scroll."
Then the pale moon grew dark, the stars shone
    out,
And Harold moved the diamond points about
Upon the blue until these words were read :—
" Lilian ! my love for you is Dead ! Dead ! Dead ! "
With that she gave a little scream,
But was rejoiced to find it all a dream.
How could she nestle thus in Harold's arms,
Like a blush rose-bud opening all her charms,
And dream such treachery of his loving heart !—
It almost made her tender conscience smart.
But on the morrow she the dream dismissed
For Harold lingeringly her lips had kissed.

" The morrow ! " Ah ! what meaning to us lies
In those two words !   The being who defies
The laws of life, sees hanging in the gloom
His dread to-morrow laden with his doom.
It may to all of us portend dismay,
For who can tell what's kernelled in the day ?
And yet we lightly tread the festive earth
As if each day endowed us with new birth,

For to our great capacity for fretting
The Lord in kindness granted quick-forgetting.

Lilian looked through her casement on the
    morrow
And found the heavens were shedding tears of
    sorrow
Upon the dismal earth. The sparrows took
Their crumbs of comfort with dejected look,
And twittered to her on the window-sill
In pitying tones : how could their hearts be still
In such a rain when Lilian was by,
Looking distressful at the weeping sky !
She was the only human friend they knew,
And to her window their wet feathers flew,
Just as in Southwold in the country air
The birds in trouble sought her tender care.
She watched the traffic rolling through the street,—
The ceaseless hurry of the busy feet,—
And saw the rags of poverty go by
Steaming with wet, and with a tender sigh
She closed the casement, dimly wondering why
The Mind which made the weeping world should be
So cruel to our weak humanity.
But as she pondered she was made aware
That Nature gave to all the boundless air,
Light, food and water, plenty for us all,

E

But laziness and self held man in thrall,
And therefore in the selfish rush for pelf
Humanity grew cruel to itself.
And then she laughed at her own puzzled mind,—
Such problems must be patent to the blind !
The world was made for all, and all are free
To make the best of what they hear and see,
For life is what we make it, and our dreams
Are ever lit from Heaven by spirit-beams.
To aid this thoughtful mood came Lady Grace,
Philosophy reflected in her face,
She having dashed up to fair Lilian's door,
Bespattering mud upon the humble poor,
With her two prancing steeds and chariot proud,
The envy of the wet pedestrian crowd.
She kissed fair Lilian on her blush-rose cheek,
And looking charmingly distressed and meek,
She talked of all the troubles of the times ;
How the poor suffered in these treacherous climes ;
How discontent prevailed and all cried " Give ! "
Instead of giving, that their souls might live
And Love be satisfied,—for if all gave
There would be none from discontent to save.
Then she told Lilian she was on her way
Her weekly visits to the poor to pay,
And tender-hearted Lilian was grieved
That she had not the same fine thought conceived,

And asked dear Lady Grace if she might be
Her help-mate in relief of misery
One happy day; for Harold would be pleased
To know that she had some poor spirit eased ;
And Grace consented with such love-lit eyes
She might have been an angel in disguise.

She might have been ! Ah ! yes ! she might have
    been !
But for the wickedness that lay unseen
Beneath that flower of human loveliness
Whose beauty it seemed sacrilege to dress,
So perfect were its lines.   It would be vain
To clothe a lily ; Beauty would be slain !
(Why did God waste this loveliness on her ?
Such natures it were best to clothe with fur !
Then we should know them with their purring ways
And never trust their soft, deceitful gaze.)
She came to Lilian to destroy her peace,
That she might Harold's fettered heart release,
And yet she did it in the name of Love,
With a soft, cooing manner like a dove,
Just as the Spring will woo a gentle flower
With sunny warmth, and in an icy hour
Kill it with wanton joy !

              The pattering rain
Was blown all night against the window-pane

In Lilian's room.   Behind her sheltering walls
She waited long,—sad as the wind that calls
Dead leaves together when warm Summer sighs
Her languid life away, and slowly dies
In Autumn's garnering arms, all wet with tears.
But Harold came not : and strange trembling fears
Crept through her nerves in phantom company ;
With all that dull, weird, strain of agony
That drears the brain, and grays the hair, and writes
The poetry that sorrow's hand indites
For all the yearning, restless human race
In lines of trouble on each speaking face.

Where did he linger ?   Was he hurt or dead ?
Why could she not one tear of sorrow shed
And wail herself away till morning light
Flushed its red gold o'er this dark dream of Night ?
She heard a creaking step upon the stair !
Was it his spirit wandering in the air ?
She dared not look ; it chilled her blood ; it felt
As though it crept up to her side and knelt !
Then came a touch ! 'twas Harold's ! and her tears
Flowed in full streams and drowned her trembling
        fears :—
" Oh ! Harold darling, I have watched the Night
Shed its wild tears until the morning light
Rubied my windows with its hopeful glow,

But I felt desolate as wastes of snow
Desolate, Harold, as when hope has fled,
As when the roses have their last bud shed,
As when I saw you in my wretched dream
Follow the Lady up the moon's cold beam.'

" Forgive me, Lilian, I have been but wild,
And I forgot my Lilian was a child,
Unversed in our ' Society's' cold ways ;
No husband by his wife for ever stays,
And I last night was by some friends allured
Who thought my gentle wife my soul immured
And cramped ; and in defence of you, my dear,
I spent the night with them without a fear."

" Alas ! Alas ! that I should be despised,
And these false friends should be more highly
    prized !
I, left alone to weep without a word,
While they your lightest play of fancy heard ;
They knew you safe, I thought you 'mongst the
    dead,
And from my heart all thought of comfort fled !
If your ' Society ' would make a wife
Suffer like this, then I despise its life,
'Tis false ; 'tis base ; but do not think me weak,
For if the clarion of war should speak,

And you were needed to defend the right,
Would I not speed you forth into the Night,
And hear unflinchingly the booming guns,
Strong as a Spartan woman with her sons?"

Kind, tender Lilian! strong, and sweet, and true,
" Society " is not for such as you ;
The mother takes her daughter to the waltz,
And bids her smile upon a heart that's false,
The husband trains his wife as a decoy,
That she may her seductive arts employ
To win him favours, honours, place, and power ;
The toady fawns and flatters hour by hour,
And murders Truth to please hard Mammon's
        eyes
Who lives on surfeits of deceits and lies.
Is there a glory in such life as this?
Can moral blindness bring us lives of bliss ?
No ! shout the noble hearts who've lived and died
To cleanse society's dark, filthy tide !
Oh ! for a wrathful cataract to sweep
Its stagnant waters down the cleansing steep !
A moral revolution to upheave
This haunt of Vanity, where all deceive !

But she was comforted ;—the gift of Love
Brings consolation like the light above,—

And ere another bitter hour had flown
Fresh flowers of Fancy in her heart had grown
Towards her Sun, her Idol, her Delight,
Her living Vision of emotions bright !
And so with her sweet spirit cleansed with tears,
With senses keen, intensified by fears,
She smiled on Harold and his sheltering arms
Unfolded to receive her tremulous charms :
And then they passed a lovelier, tenderer hour
Than souls have e'er enjoyed since Eden's bower
Thrust its heart treasures on the weeping earth
To bless her valleys with a human birth.

Who would not quarrel to re-live again
Love's keen emotions by inertia slain ?

Alas ! for Harold with his web of sin
Encircling, netting his poor body in !
Grace had been with him on that night of
    death !
And he had kissed her with his plighted breath !
While Lilian struggled in that gust of tears
Drearily haunted with her heart-made fears.
      See in the Night-black heavens
        A portent red,
      A heart with tears of blood,
        For Love's sake shed !

Speared by a shaft of gold—
An arrow bright,—
Which sought the sunlit heavens,
But found the Night !

Just two days after this the Lady came,
With her bright eyes on fire and cheeks aflame,
To take dear Lilian to the troubled poor,
Lazily charioted from door to door.
Sad sights they saw : weak faces stained by drink,
And feeble creatures trembling on the brink
Of vast eternity ; hearts torn by care
And others happy as the summer air
In spite of portents of impending woe
Which their high spirits fain would overthrow ;
But worst of all, crime pressed its blood-red hand
On poverty's dry throat, and spoilt the grand
Conception, born amid the suffering poor,
That God will bless the hardships men endure.
(Crime 'gainst this rule rebels and would defy
The message telephoned from God on high.)
That poverty breeds genius, hope breeds joy,
And aspirations tremble in the poorest boy,
We know full well.   But all this sore distress
In homes without a dream of loveliness
Or touch of beauty (save the sad, sweet eyes
Of broken-hearted mothers torn by cries

Of tender children famishing for food),
Made gentle Lilian pitifully brood.
And when they came to one whose golden hair
Streamed o'er her pillow like a vision rare,
And made a background for the loveliest face
That Nature's skilful hand could ever trace,
She felt as hopeless as the last fond sigh
Of dying summer.   Death seemed standing by
Ready to bear the body to the tomb ;
But the faint spirit shone out through the gloom
To tell its woeful tale ere she was gone ;
And Lilian listened silent as a stone.

"O World ! my heart is dying, but Life's song
That haunts my mem'ry, Love would fain prolong,
For He inspired it in an hour of Spring,
Ere I had dreamed of all this sorrowing.
I loved the fields, the woods, the open air,
And lived from hour to hour without a care ;
Like a wild bird I roamed, and like a bee
I sought the stores of honied secrecy
That Nature yields to all who love her well,
And fall unconsciously beneath her spell.
And God was with me then ; in all the flowers
(Those beauteous dreamings of the sunlit hours,)
He looked at me.   The Wind was but His breath,
Blowing fresh life amid the mists of Death.

The stars were but His eyes, and 'neath His
    dome
Of blue at night, I pictured Heaven my home.
And one day He came nearer to me still,
And spoke to me with Love's magnetic thrill
In the soft breathings of a youth divine
In whose dear features goodness seemed to shine.
Where is God now?   And where that voice so
    sweet
That every evening in the woods would greet
My listening ears?   Has not God left the world
And Love's wild flame into Hell's furnace hurled?
Oh! can you not discern Him?   Speak to me!
Bring from that room my baby mystery
Cradled in sleep.   Then p'raps my love will live
And I shall see my God again and give
Him praise and honour."   Lady Grace arose
And brought the baby buried in repose,
And laid it in the yearning mother's arms ;
Then the sweet babe awoke and laughed its charms
Out of its two blue eyes.   The mother's face
Soon rippled o'er with smiles, the gloom to chase ;
The heart was light again tho' Death was near.

" Now can I see the Lord again appear !
He smiles at me !   See ! in those love-lit eyes
He lives ! lovelier than flowers, or starry skies,

Or woods, or streams, when painted by the sun
In summer pictures, exquisitely done ;
One glimpse of man's intelligence is worth
The gathered riches of material Earth !
Oh ! God ! forgive my infidelity,
And waft my soul across th' ethereal sea
Into the fulness of eternity.
My lover must be dead : he gave me this
Memento of our hours of tender bliss.
He could not leave me sorrowing here alone
In sight of God's most awful Judgment Throne.
He must have gone before me, and I may
Be with him yet upon the Judgment Day.
Look ! Lady Grace, are not those Harold's eyes ?
Are not they blue like thoughts of Paradise ?
Smile ! baby, smile ! you cannot e'er appear
Lovelier than Harold did to me, my dear.
But he has gone, and I am dying fast,
And when the shroud of Night o'er me is cast
I shall have faded like a flower full-blown
And only Death will love me as his own."

Then Lilian, trembling, walked across the room
And touched the baby fingers in the gloom,
And lit the light, and saw the lovely blue
That only Harold's darling eyes e'er knew ;
And Love—that mute detective—further saw

In the deep blue a tiny speck, a flaw,
That her own Harold's had, and then she said :—

" Who was your sweet one whom you fancy dead,
My suffering sister ? p'raps we yet may find
Him longing for his baby left behind
To praise his Maker in the midst of woe."
Then the salt tears began to overflow
Adown the sufferer's cheeks, and then she told
Our Harold's history, till her limbs grew cold
And Death enveloped her, and slowly stilled
The voice that froze fair Lilian's blood, and chilled
Her love for Harold.

       Thus fair Lilian met
As if by accident his country pet,
His faithful Mary, his contented slave,
Who would have killed the slandering knave
Who dared to speak one word against her joy ;
For Love when pure admits of no alloy
And worships ever though its heart be torn
With wounded feelings delicately borne.

As breaks the storm-cloud o'er the mountain
    height,
As Summer withers in the frost of night,
As lilies die when broken at the stem,

Though torn by Love to weave a diadem,
So o'erwrought Lilian by that death-bed fell,
Plunged in a grief of which no words can tell
The bitterness, the torment, and the woe ;
E'en Grace's tears began to overflow
Watching the baby playing with the dead,
Tossing the hair about the silent head,
And saying " Peep-Bo " to the death-shut eyes :
She tore the child away and hushed its cries,
Then turned to Lilian, who from faint despair
She brought to life again with fresh-fanned air.

Ah ! Lady Grace, you never thought to see
Death carry Mary to eternity
And stamp his signet on your treachery !
It would have pleased your heart to watch her
    eyes
Shine out on Lilian with a mad surprise ;
To watch hot jealousy with pulsing thud
Like smothered steam course thro' her bounding
    blood ;
To see wild passion surge up thro' her throat
And hear the scalding vap'rous words up float ;
But to be baulked by Death of all this glee
Was never part of your fine treachery.
No secret now ! for all the world must know
How your false heart had planned this cruel blow

For trustful Lilian!   The hurrying wind
Brushed past the window where her heart had
    sinned
And seemed to carry on its tell-tale breath
The news to Harold on the wings of Death.

And Lilian took the baby in her arms
And pitied it, still wondering at its charms :—
"You might have spared my heart, my Lady Grace,
The darts that pierce it through this baby face,
You are a bitter woman, with a spite
As secret as the workings of the Night.
Now is your scheming heart to me laid bare,
And never more can ye be Lady Fair,
But a black-hearted horror! sly, like mice,
With heart corrupt congealed in breasts of ice.
Can meanness hide behind a noble name ?
Your ghostly ancestors must blush for shame
At this your petty spite !   Why have you stung,
You wasp ?   Has my unthinking, foolish tongue
Wrought evil in your path ? or do you sting
Only for pleasure like a gnat-made thing ?
Or is it worse ?   Oh ! horror !   Is it worse ?
Are you my Harold's too ?   Does envy curse
Your coal-black heart? and would you therefore kill,
Stab, sting your rival ?   Nay ! the thought must
    flee !

Harold of you could never amorous be !
A soul that's cynical Love cannot grieve,
And Sorrow would not one pure tear-drop leave
Within thy greedy eyes. Away ! False friend !
You've strived to break my heart, and gained
    your end."
Then with hysteria laughing through her pain,
And wild-eyed fever mounting to her brain,
She turned with sudden interest to the child,
And with these words its fretfulness beguiled :
" But, baby, you are innocent of all,
A merry cypher, product of the fall
Of two weak hearts into Love's melting fire ;
Just a sweet outcome of a wild desire :
But how could Harold leave you here to die,
Sweet, laughing baby, can you tell me why ?
Is he a fickle father, think you, dear ?
A man at whom a wanton eye might leer
And draw him like a magnet ?   Is he such ?
If so, I cannot glory now in much.
But he shall see you, baby, he shall hear
Your pretty prattle, and when you appear
The heart of heaven may open : we may see
Great truths behind Love's veil of mystery."

These frenzied words, unnatural, untrue,
To Lilian's lips, tormentingly upflew,

And stung my Lady Grace ; Lilian, so kind,
Could not be e'en by jealousy made blind
To all the human trouble of the scene ;
She could not love the baby much, I ween !

But Lady Grace stept forth and barred the way,
And said : "You taunt me, Madam, but I'll pay
Your words with interest and taunt you too.
I grieve at all this passion.   Is it you,
Fair Lilian,—so good, so true, so kind,—
To be thus tossed about by passion blind ?
Should you who love Humanity so well,
Breathe burning language eloquent of Hell ?
Why should you sully your sweet lips with words
Which would have scared your friendly twittering
      birds ?
You are so good, you know ; so unconcerned
About the evils human hearts have learned.
Was it not kind of me to ope your eyes,
To bare your lover's heart of its disguise,
That ye might learn a lesson lying deep
In poverty's spare bosom lulled to sleep ?
I thought you'd like a visit to the poor
That you might see the troubles they endure."

"Oh ! heart of Death ! Silence your ill-formed
      jeers,"

Said Lilian ;—" My cheeks are cut with tears ;
You've torn my budding heart ; and taught me more
In one sad hour than youth should e'er explore ;
Be satisfied ; my eyes are opened wide ;
I find it may be hell to be a bride ;
To wed impurity, to kiss its lips
Is worse than scourging with a hundred whips.
Your words are true ; it surely cannot be
That I, so simple, burn with jealousy
And rave like Hell !   I must be sadly changed ;
My heart o'er wild, weird melodies has ranged
With sudden inspiration ; I am lost ;
For a great wave my anguished heart has tossed
A wreck upon Life's shore in blinding mist.
A devil passed my ear just now and hissed
Fierce scorn at this sweet baby ; must I hate
This pretty mould of flesh because hard fate
Has given it to a wanton ?   Yes ; I must ;
I cannot now my better feelings trust ;
I loathe you, baby ; I will lay you here,
And leave you shivering, without a tear ;
I cannot touch you ; you are not my own ;

.   .   .   .   .   .

How can I speak in thus untender tone ?
Some other heart within my breast has grown
In one short hour !   Oh ! let a wild remorse
Tear at your scheming heart and thus divorce

F

The devil from you, bitter, biting Grace !
I would from memory blot out your face.
But, baby, I relent ; I still will be
A woman full of warm humanity ;
So let us pass, my Lady, let us go ;
You've trodden rudely on unsullied snow."

And so the baby in fair Lilian's arms
Passed out into the world with wild alarms
Ringing in Lilian's ears.   She hailed a cab,—
For pride made in her heart too deep a stab,
To let her sit by Lady Grace's side ;—
The space 'twixt good and evil must be wide.

She found her husband anxious in his home,
Alarmed to find his darling did not come,
He waited long ; the dreary hours went by
Until Night's veil slid down the sunset sky,
And Lilian came not.   Conscience seemed to say
That he deserved to be chastised this way
For his past conduct ; but it would be mean
To think such petty spite of his pure queen.
He heard the cab, the bell, and rushed to greet
His darling's entry from the busy street ;
He tried to kiss her, but she waved him off,
And tendered him the baby with a scoff ;—
" This is your child, your Mary's child,

I know all now, my brain is nearly wild,"
She swiftly said ; " In this poor street you'll see
 (*giving him a card*)
Your Mary gazing at eternity.
Go, man, and bury her ; it is her due ;
The final service she can ask of you."

Harold stood livid 'gainst the whitened wall,
Pained by the shock ; for he could not recall
Rough words from Lilian in the happy past ;
But now it seemed as though hard stones were
 cast
Against his tender face by pure white hands ;
As though the hall were filled with harsh brass
 bands
Torturing with full-inflated murd'rous lung
The tenderest melodies the gods have sung.

The baby laughed at him and strove to fly
Into his arms ; and Lilian, with a sigh,
Gave it to Harold, while her eyes grew dim
With tears still eloquent of love for him.
She left the baby then and sought her room,
Feeling o'ershadowed by some awful doom ;
She tore away the diamonds from her ears,
Took off the brooch his mother wore for years,
Her rings most costly and her bracelets too,—

But round her wedding-ring sweet fancies flew ;
It was her golden rosary of Love,
On which she told soft prayers to Heaven above,
And breathed her sacred kisses ; it would rim
Her thoughts in black for ever, if to him
She were one moment faithless while she wore
The hallowed emblem of the love he bore ;—
To part with that meant loving nevermore.
So it was kept ; but all the rest were piled
Into a heap, from which bright fairies smiled
In twinkles through the little jewelled eyes,—
Aiding the charm that in a keepsake lies.
They were his gifts, soiled by his touch impure,
She would not wear them till she found a cure
To heal with gentle hand the cutting smart
That seemed to penetrate her very heart.
Fevered with passion, pained with wounded pride,
She walked the room with wild indignant stride,
And then resolved to seek her father's help
To save her from the curse of wounded self.

Harold was dazed : he knew not what to do
When up the stairs his maddened Lilian flew ;
With fervent heart he wished the flight could be
To heaven ! away from all this misery.
Try how he would he could not wash away
The stains that tarnished his wild life,—called "gay."

Fain would he be light-hearted ; but a weight
Depressed his spirit with a force as great
As waters infinite.   *Now* she knew all ;
The secret of his brutal passion fall
Into the sensual pit of low desire,
Ere he had seen the blaze of Heavenly fire
That shone from Love's high beacon by the sea :
Would he had told her all his misery
When in the lap of Southwold they were shown
Visions of glory few fond hearts have known :
A woman would have gauged a woman's heart
And taught him how to smooth poor Mary's part.
Yet who could talk to innocence of guilt ?
'Twould be like plunging to the very hilt
A murderous sword in human blood : No ! No !
It seemed impossible to stay the blow :
Now he must face his sorrow-stricken wife
Conscious of having soiled her pure, white life.

With leaden feet he followed up the flight
Lilian had touched with feet as swift as light,
And 'neath her blazing eye and burning cheek
He stood convicted : conscience made him weak ;
And Lilian seemed to toss him to and fro
Like a lone boat in a Pacific blow
In her wild flood of words :—

"I am undone!
Deceived! I thought in you my love had won
The pure devotion of a noble mind
That I could worship.   Truly Love is blind!
I would unwrite your name upon my heart
But Law forbids it, taking sorry part
With Man 'gainst Woman! Oh! the brutal thought!
You came to me impure and o'er me wrought
The spell of love ; had I but done the same
To you, you would have rightly cursed my name.
Oh! free of heart!   Oh! libertine of Love!
Oh! hypocrite to talk to Heaven above!
To tell me that you would a prism be
So that I might your heart more clearly see!
How I could laugh at my credulity,
But it were best to weep at Man's deceit!
The knees that knelt in homage at my feet
Had stooped to win a wanton ere they came
To worship me !   The eyes that lit Love's flame
Were like two beacons of deceitful light
Luring a vessel on the rocks at Night!
The lips that kissed the wanton came to mine
And touched them simulating Love divine!
As tho' a man could stand and worship God
And then leer round to give the Devil a nod!
He that loves wantons must with wantons dwell,
For innocence can never live in Hell.

'Tis cowardly to seek a pure-eyed bride
And taint her with the guilt you fain would hide.
Oh ! fool, to trick me !   Fool, to give me cause
To cavil at Man's Woman-trampling laws !
Fool, to conceive that purity could be
Happily wedded to impurity !
See how the fates have worked !   See how your
    friends
Have laughed to watch how good with evil blends !
See how your scheming Lady Grace has sought
To bring our nuptial happiness to naught !
How subtly she has planned with secret aim
To stamp me with the taint of all your shame !
Death came between us or you would have
    known
The hate your Mary would to you have shown :
All your deceit would then have seen the day.
How could you take your Mary, young and gay,
Into your heart, and treat her as your queen,
Then leave her helpless with no board between
Her and a gaping Hell ?   You never cared
How your poor Mary through temptation fared
After you left her ; yet she was your slave,
And happily the great world's tidal wave
Laid her upon the sands of Time unharmed,
And when she died she was for you alarmed,
Not for herself : and so she well might be,

You frozen unit of Humanity !
What, pray, may I expect from such a man ?
Homage ?   Joy?   Love ?   Yes, for a moment's
    span,
But not for ever.   If my beauty hide
Itself to try you, would your faith abide ?
No ; for already Lady Grace has been
A welcome guest within your heart unseen.
Ah ! you may start ! but tho' I have not known
The false flowers in a London ball-room blown,
Still I know well a jealous woman's eye,
However subtle it may be or sly."

At this she ceased, and it was sad to see
The lovely lady's bitter agony ;
Her tender eyes of blue with passion flashed
And all her body seemed with fury lashed ;
She was transfigured from a gentle girl
To a majestic angel who could hurl
A mighty avalanche of righteous wrath,—
The gentle South had changed to gusty North.

" Be gentle, Lilian," wretched Harold said,
" Hurl not your fury on my helpless head ;
Be kind ; for I am broken down with grief
To think that Love can bring me no relief.
He that soils Purity has guilt so great

That Heaven itself cannot avert the fate
That he must justly suffer.   I am dyed
With guilt : Mary I loved not ; yet I lied
My love to her, and she believed me true,
But it was not until I met with you
That I felt Love's soft magic of the soul,
Which from my being all contentment stole
Until I won you.   Is there in the skies
No quick forgiveness when Repentance cries?
Thousands have treated women just the same
Though my lips speak it to their deathless shame ! "
Then Lilian relented and with sighs
Spoke her heart's agonizing cries ;
She looked just like a lily in despair,
No more rejoicing in the Earth's sweet air,
But ripe for spirit-land.   Black rings appeared
Beneath her eyes, signals of danger reared
By mortal trouble of the heart within :—
Her beauty seemed receding from his sin :—
She sat her down exhausted on the bed
And   with   soft   pantings   these   heart-yearnings
    said :—

" Oh ! that my Spirit-Lord would tear away
The knowledge that this too malignant day
Has scorched into my brain.   Alas !   I *know !*
And must for ever *know*.   The winds that blow

Will whisper it or howl it in my ear,
And grinning Death will bear it to my bier ;
The sun will smile it sadly down to me,
And moons will shed it o'er the whisp'ring sea !
I feel as though the idol that I reared
Had been all suddenly with mud besmeared
By treacherous hands, and try howe'er I may
I cannot wash the hateful stains away.

.   .   .   .   .   .

" But, Harold, dear, I am a woman still,
And I must love you e'en against my will,
My broken idol shall be dear to me,
E'en as my old, soiled doll in infancy
Was dearer far than new ones finely dressed,
And far more lovingly by me caressed.
Nature to all some compensation brings
To soothe Life's ever-agonizing strings.
Oh !   Harold, we can never feel again
Those Southwold dreamings in the sun and rain ;
They would be diff'rent now ; but still we might
Have others bringing lovelier delight ;
More human, p'raps ! more tender, being born
Of gentle grief, too constant, like each morn.
Some change seems wrought within me, something
        great,
I seem exalted to a higher state ;
And yet I feel so weak, my Harold dear,

As though some cord had broken rather near
My beating heart ; and yet that works the same,
Flooding my being with Life's liquid flame :

. . . . . .

" So weak am I, my Harold, that my hands
Will not obey their royal queen's commands,
P'raps you will aid me, darling, to undress
That I may my reviving bed caress."

Then Lilian drooping like a dying rose
Was laid upon her pillow to repose
Breathing soft words :—" I shall not surely die,
My Harold, dear, I have no wings to fly
To spirit-land with yet ; " but Harold kissed
The words upon her lips and never wist
What they might mean until she gently said :—
" Saw you that lovely vision o'er my head ?
Harold, my sweet, it was not of the earth,
It seemed to have a wondrous spirit-birth ;
Look ! there's another, darling ; after all
There is a God ! and if He on me call
I fain must follow, for e'en stars obey
His mandate." Thus all night she dreaming lay
Talking to Harold, whom she would not pain
With too abrupt a flight to Heaven's high plain.
But when God called her, thro' the Mist she went,
Ere the dark Night had with the Morning blent,

And the last words upon her lips were clear,—
" Be kind to Mary's baby, Harold dear,
Keep him so pure, that there may be no stain
To mar his joy when Love comes round again."
With this she died ; snapped were the tender
    strings
That bound her spirit to material things.

There is no more to say : it would be vain
To sermonize upon poor Harold's pain,—
It is a book itself, and speaks to all,—
Yet there are some sweet words we would recall
Ere this Life-poem fadeth to its close,—-
" He that is pure, is lovelier than the rose."

MY LADY LOVE.

HER EYES.

LIKE wells of water, deep and calm,
    The blue of Heaven reflecting,
Her eyes with melancholy charm,
    As if my soul detecting,
Would gaze their depths into mine own ;
Two wells of Love for me alone.

And yet I felt tho' calm their gaze,
    They might be stirred to madness,
Or tremulous with passion blaze
    Into tumultuous gladness,
Or tragic with tempestuous rage,
Thrill truth into a book-bound sage.

Sometimes from out that slumbering blue,
    I've seen a torrent streaming,—
As silently as sky-born dew
    Doth set the rose-buds dreaming,—
In tears distilling human grief,
To God, the Father, for relief.

No line could plumb their depths of woe,
    When moist with floods of sorrow,
No painter catch the fitful glow
    That on some joyous morrow
Might twinkle o'er their laughing sheen,
In wild delight at thoughts unseen.

I cannot think those eyes can die
    And leave me unbefriended ;
Such lights must gem the starry sky,
    When their earth-life is ended,
And everlastingly appeal
To my tired spirit, when I feel

Distressed at all the webs of thought
    Inwoven in my being,
Sometimes like gossamer light-wrought,
    With every wind agreeing,
And sometimes like a rope to knell
Death's ever sad mysterious bell.

Her eyes, like fire, would burn that rope,
    Ere the wild knell had sounded,
And pierce me with a beam of hope,
    Though by despair surrounded,

So in their gaze as in a shrine,
My soul shall picture things divine.

Her Hair.

Take all the richest shades of red,
   And mix with russet brown,
And then conceive a texture soft
   As finest eider-down,
And deck with million glints of gold ;
Then Fancy may her hair behold.

A colour rarest of the rare,
   But ne'er forgot when seen,
A glimpse of autumn when the woods
   Are painting out their green,
And leaves indulge in wild excess,
Their dying thoughts of loveliness.

It seemed to ripple like a stream,
   When o'er her arms it fell,
Its silent cataracts of gold
   Held by some magic spell,
From bounding earthward out of sight
In paroxysms of delight.

And yet it seemed to glow with warmth,
    And on a wintry day,
Like summer breathing through the house,
    It thawed the cold away ;
With falling cascades all on fire,
What magic could she more desire ?

And then, too, by that dimpled stream,
    Two violets of blue,
In modesty did dwell alway,
    And shyly peep at you ;
Those flowers and that golden stream,
Were every maiden's envious dream.

In love-chains it would weave itself,
    And twine around my form,
More close than honeysuckle clings,
    When wondering at the storm.
She was my anchor, and her hair,
My love-wove cable, rich and rare.

And she had tiny ringlets too,
    Like little dancing sprites,
Who seemed to play a thousand tricks,
    Within her hair o' nights,
When in the lamplight they would dance
And then evade my eager glance.

And sometimes in the blue of night,
   I make two stars her eyes,
And trace her streaming hair along
   The deep, mysterious skies,
Where old astrologers have wrought
Wild theories in frenzied thought.

She was a saint by Nature made,
   Endowed from babyhood,
With that bright halo painters use,
   To crown the great and good.
Around her head it seemed to shine
As natural as things divine.

But when the gold turns silver-gray,
   Will Winter then prevail ?
Will all the woods be drear and bare
   And hushed the nightingale ?
Will her dear hair, now worth fine gold,
Be then for silver-value sold ?

Ah ! no ; for ever there will be
   A summer in her soul,
And the delightful tints of gray,
   Will sanctify the whole ;
The fields are bleached each autumn morn
As Nature ripeneth the corn.

G

Her Lips.

I have a rose in the garden,
    Blushing a delicate red,
And the bees go there marauding
    Before its bloom is shed,
As a fiend would rifle virtue ere the grace of Youth
      is fled.

But I know a flower more lovely
    Than ever a garden grew,
More delicate in complexion
    Than rose-leaf ever knew ;
And the fiend who touched it lightly would much
      his boldness rue.

Yet I have been bold to rashness,
    And tasted a hundred sips
Of the most delicious honey,
    From that flower's sacred lips ;
And she never thought I was a fiend to scorpion
      with whips.

But she shot me a golden ~~quiver~~, *arrow*
    From that vermeil Cupid bow,
As she drew her lips asunder
    To dart her witty blow ;
And I would not be half so gay if she did not
    wound me so.

Her lips made perfect language,
    They were eloquent at rest,
But when they were in motion,
    All listeners forward pressed,
That with music of her falling words, their ears
    might be caressed.

And I have seen her pouting
    Like a flower partly blown,
And nothing would the pout dissolve
    But a kiss—most lightly thrown
From the bristly lips of the man she loves to pet,
    and scold, and own.

When Love on her lips would linger
    Entranced in summer-born smiles,
None could escape the contagion
    Of all her innocent wiles ;
Round such an expanding enchantment, the world
    would blossom for miles.

But the highest aim of beauty
　　Is embodiment of Truth,
And of that her lips so rosy
　　Have been oracles from youth,
And I would sooner trust her word than anything
　　forsooth.

Yea more,—her word I've trusted,
　　She has whispered it to me,
And that breath of Truth went circling
　　Upwards to Heaven's blue sea
Where it inspires Love's sacred harp with her true
　　heart's melody.

HER AFFECTION.

Is she heartless ?　Can I say
　　Who am deluged with her love ?
She, as warm as summer ray
　　Shot from out the skies above.

Would you cut a saint in two
　　To dissect some trifling faults,
If you knew her love for you
　　Grew with jealousy's assaults ?

Is she heartless?   Well, last eve
  I felt such a depth of bliss
That I thought ne'er more to grieve
  She might hesitate to kiss.

Yet 'twixt now and that fair then
  Some vile harpy to her came
Whispering lies that this, my pen,
  Should not write against my fame.

Told her how in some wild street
  I had met a maiden fair, ·
Had embraced her, called her " Sweet,"
  Kissed her in the open air,

On some night while she, his Love,
  Waited in her chamber lone,
For his presence, as a dove
  Waits to have its love-food thrown.

So to-night, when my heart called
  On my lady in her room,
Her cold looks my eyes appalled
  Casting all my soul in gloom.

Lies seemed circling in the air,
  Tearing in their spite her face,
All seemed ugly, nothing fair,
  And I felt unknown disgrace.

Shivering me with icy gaze,
   As a cloud doth gray the morn,
Then enkindling in a blaze
   Of unutterable scorn.

Oh ! I knew those tranquil eyes
   Could be fired at any wrong,
Could not favour cant or lies,
   Would not brook injustice long.

Like a river wide and cold,
   Anger rolled our souls between,
She upon her bank looked bold,
   I looked trembling on the scene.

Words were thrown from either bank,
   Passion gleaming from her eye,
But I had my God to thank,
   Truth must ever drown a lie.

So the mountain of her love
   Soon upheaved a spring of tears,
Sweeping from the heights above
   Drowning all the lies and fears.

And we loved each other more
   For the lies that had been told,
Till Love seemed a vaster store
   Than Eternity could hold.

Poets who exist have felt
    Human passion deeply stirred,
No musician would have knelt
    In the worship of the Lord,

If his heart had dormant lain
    In a bosom ribbed with ice,
Or with all his passion slain
    In the slavery of vice.

So, my lady, poet-born,
    Is an ecstasy divine,
Has a heart that can be torn
    By the grief that enters thine.

How can she be heartless, then ?
    She, a passion-breathing soul,
Heaven's angelic denizen,
    Tender, loving, perfect, whole.

HER RELIGION.

It was a season of great happiness,
    A summer-time of Love, of which birds sing
In nooks of green, when suns shine shadowless
    Of cloud, or mist, or other lurid thing ;
A time of peace ; as though pale, freakish
    Death,

Had thrust us into Heaven unrestrained,
Or otherwise had glorified our breath,
While our full, sensuous bodies on the Earth
remained.

As rose-trees lift their buds to kiss the sun,
So all the budding flowers of her mind
Blossomed towards me, and there was not one
Of all the maids of Earth, whom Love could
find
More worthy of those gifts which he could give
In ever-varying fancy, like a rainbow-shower ;
Love knew no maiden worthier to live,
Or any bed that had a sweeter dower
Than that which did in fear, her snowy limbs
embower.

Love painted smiles upon her ; not such smiles
As maidens make to order in their youth,
When softly favouring their mothers' wiles,
But smiles all radiant with the blush of
Truth ;
And in her noon-tide altitudes of Thought,
Her lips would ofttimes tremble into song
More rare than nightingales have ever wrought
Amid inspiring branches, while the throng
Of heedless warblers sleep till day shall come along.

And I would listen as a wondering child
   Doth magnify her dear, old grandame's tales
Of woe and love, when she may be beguiled,
   (Though all protesting that her memory fails,)
To tell the tender passions of those days
   When Hope rained gold and Life leapt up in
      flame:
I heard her sing one eve this Hymn of Praise
   To the Great Heart of Love, whose mighty
      name
Would more attract her than high pinnacles of
   Fame.

HYMN TO THE GREAT HEART OF LOVE.

   " OH ! thou great Heart of Love !
Our passions vary, like a weaver's loom,
   The threads of life,
We know not e'en the pattern of our doom,
   Or what our strife,
Yet, though the Hiding Veil cannot be rent,
The throbs of thy Great Heart make us
   content.

   " Yet discontent abounds !
The wind from out the North doth woo
   the South
     To warm its breath,

And Northward blows the breeze from
        South's warm mouth,
    Tho' it mean death ;
Autumn in Winter fades, and then fresh
        Spring
Doth lead fair Summer to the harvesting.

    " Change, change, all things do change !
Yet the wide throb of thy Great Heart,
        Oh ! Love !
        Remains the same,
By thee we feel there is a God above,
        Who knows our shame,
    And yet forgives us for thine own sweet sake ;
    And our *hearts'* tribute only will He take."

And once as flames yearn upward to the sky,
    And gorse doth blaze its passion to the sun,
My loved one, tortured by a pulpit lie,
    Rose, as a suppliant to the Holy One
In church ; amid the silence of the choir,
    With tongue triumphant in melodious prose,
She winged the congregation's thoughts up
        higher
    Than e'er the consecrated priest's words rose,
Who wrapped his spirit life in vestment, form
        and pose.

ORATION IN CHURCH.

" Is there a Devil, think you ? if so, where ?
    And have you met and bowed to him ?
  Or seen him floating in the ambient air ?
  Or has he caught you by your nether limb
    And made you swear
  That God and all things holy shall be
    brought
    Into his blazing, desolating snare ?

" The Christian zealot keeps his Majesty
    embalmed
    In words of Holy Writ,
  That no poor soul should ever be becalmed
    Or have one whit
  Of ease, lest he be damned
  By easy negligence of this wide fact,
  That Satan doth inhabit all this tract
    Of earth, and we are jammed
      Betwixt a God above,
  And some wild Being, never born for love.

" Why should we swallow this un-Christlike
    thought ?
    Making our God both wicked and unkind,

He could not have for us this scare-crow
  wrought,
 As we a hawk create, to fright and blind
 The little birds that devastate the field,
And for the love of life would steal our
  harvest yield.

" This mystery of Evil who can gauge?
  Spread through the tale of life
 From infancy to age :
 Whence cometh all this hidden strife?
 Who gave vitality to such a thing?
 That doth so surely circulate and sting
   Through all our being,
   With strange soliciting,
  Far greater than the swirl
 Of some hot whirlpool whose revolving flood
  Doth onward hurl
 The fascinated soul, whose heated blood
 Doth love to revel in the constant whirl.

" And when the vortex comes :—What then?
  Oblivion ?
 No ! No ! a thunderous No ! comes from
   the mountain glen
  And fruitful river bank ;

E'en flowers bend their heads and smile
    derision,
And timid birds look up and thank
Their Maker for their length of vision
While poor short-sighted man
Thinks he discerns the end of Life's
    ambition !

" He that made Good made Evil ; Why ?
Because there is an opposite to every truth,
    To old age,—youth :
If there be Death there must be Life ;
    If Peace,—Strife ;
But they who made the Devil were monks and
    fools,
Who thought it fun to frighten all the
    schools."

They let her speak thus far, and then all faint,
    Her spirit died within her ; 'twas too much
For mortal frame to harbour such a saint,
    Who was in close and sympathetic touch
With things of mystery, beyond our ken ;
    Born an immortal in a mortal mould,
She almost carried you to Heaven, when
    With eyes on fire she would her mind unfold
In rich embroidery of words, ne'er over-bold.

Ah me ! how good, how tender—true she is !
  How like a star in watchful gentleness,
Shining afar out of a blue abyss
  Of purity ! a creature born to bless
The reeking millions with her sainted breath :
  The tender priest came from his pulpit-throne,
Like a dethronèd king and fought with Death,
  That Earth its white flower by the God-wind
    sown
Might rear into the fruit of promise, fully blown.

She soon revived, and then the priest was mute
  With adoration of her saint-like eyes
And halo-forming hair, until a flute
  Spoke from the organ trilling to the skies,
With seventh resolving on a tonic boom
  Of softly thundering pedal ; then said he :—
" This organ minstrelsy, 'mid sacred gloom,
  Is like the spreading of the soul when free,
Into the heights and depths of Love's great
    mystery."

I saw he loved her, and forgave her lips
  Their wild oration, which they did not
    make
Until God's blessing, through his finger-tips,
  Had passed among the people ; then she break

The mystic hush of people's silent prayers,
  With wonder-stirring words, first weak, then
    flushed
With flight of passion up the aerial stairs
Of Fancy's palace ; thus the crowd, all hushed,
  Listened, until her rose-life drooped, all   faint
    and crushed.

'Twas sad but beautiful, and seemed most mad
  To all except the cultured and the kind ;
She knew no creed but Love, and therefore had
  A wise abhorrence of devotion blind
In consecrated buildings, priests, or forms,
  Candles or incense, which promoted strife ;
And   hated,   too,   the   canting   pride   which
    storms
  At kneeling postures, and is much too rife,—
With her, life was religion, not religion, life.

WESTMINSTER ABBEY.

A Dream.

Thou Sacred Shrine of Truth,
Lit with the morning twilight of our Nation's
        Youth !
    How oft before thee in a mist of thought
    Have I fair fancies tenderly inwrought
        Within thy graceful form !
A haven pictured thee amid this world of storm ;

    Thought thee a flower in stone,
In bud a thousand years and yet not fully blown,
    For ever freshened by thy Nation's tears
    To newer beauties thro' the garnering years
        So that fair Nature might
Be some day wildly envious of the lovely sight.

    Here baby-fingers lie
That grasped eternal life in their Death agony,
    And rose-lips withered 'neath thy stones lie hid,
    And mighty brains which gathered strength amid

War, Fire, Storm, Fear, and Flood,
Lie mouldering silent here with Princes of the Blood.

A temple of the Kings
And gods of men, who soared upon the mighty
wings
Of wild ambition, fearless as the birds,
Some gifted with o'erpowering wealth of words
That held the world in chains
Of iron slav'ry to their busy-thoughtèd brains.

Here souls of music rest,
Whose plaintive anthems still go sobbing through
thy breast,
Breaking through tears in " Hallelujahs " wild
At the remembrance of that God-sent Child
Who taught all hearts to love
Peace, Honour, Truth, Love, Wisdom, and the
Light above.

Here poets, too, are found,
Whose magic words of Truth still trumpet forth
their sound,
But some, alas ! lie dead amongst their bones
With elegies self-written in false tones,
Which—never following Truth—
Sought artificial aids to gain immortal Youth.

H

Here sculptors, too, lie dead,
Who mused in marble with poetic eye, and shed
　A glory into things inanimate,
　And made stone speak of love and fiercest
　　hate,
　　And clay portray a grace
To be for aye a marvel to the living race.

　A Homer gazing out
With stony eyes upon the busy world about ;
　A Pitt transmuted into stony wrath,
　While Fox in marble eloquence speaks forth,
　　Are ever sad to see :
A sculptor's life must aye most melancholy be :

　Cold his most passionate form,
Though floating through his charmèd brain ideals
　　warm
　Will glow his Fancy into fever-heat,
　And make him dream stone-pictures passing
　　sweet,
　　Which shall his name adorn
When his small world has passed into that Mist
　forlorn.

　And on thy Abbey walls
His melancholy work the pensive soul enthrals,

Making it blossom as his own mind did
At the sweet touch of Fancy all unbid,
  Until we float above
Into ethereal regions of Immortal Love.

  One night I lingered long
After the sweet-voiced choir had sung their evensong,
  Gazing enraptured at a sculptured face
  While choir and people slowly left the place,
    And I all unaware
Was wrapped in sacred darkness from the worldly
    air.

  I saw the sculptured eyes
Light up with human feeling in a wild surprise,
  The limbs moved slowly with awakened life
  And all the Abbey with new joy was rife,
    And then I saw descend
The sculptured Kings of men, in social life to blend.

  Outside across the sky
Electric messages of love did swiftly fly
  In those mysterious meteors of fire,
  To summon angels to the Abbey choir,
    Where they might see a sight
More wondrous than enchantments in a dream at
    night.

First Purcell did descend,
And to his lovèd organ-loft his way did wend,
　To charm the Night with soul-beseeching chords
　More tender than the breath of chosen words
　　By sweetest poet sung
After some poignant grief his gentle heart hath
　　wrung.

　　Purcell's deep soul was wrought
By Music's subtle charms to fine creative thought,
　When Handel, listening to that god of song,
　Was drawn to life again and walked along
　　To where the Master played,
And like a modest pupil tendered him his aid.

　　At the old Master's word,
He moved the organ-stops, and all in wonder heard
　The pastoral " hautboy " and the trilling " flute,"
　Soft " dulciana," and the voice acute
　　Of " trumpets " wildly blown,
Played by the greatest master of harmonious tone.

　　At first with prelude quaint,
Like a despondent lover making sweet complaint,
　He wooed the air, and then with might of love
　His ardent music sought the Heaven above,

Till through the roof there came
A garland of bright cherubs, rosy cheeks aflame.

These were the gentle boys
Who died like tender snowdrops in their Spring-
      tide joys,
  And took their voices from the Abbey choir
  To swell the anthem in a region higher
    Where all do worship God,
And not their own weak fancies, crying " Ichabod."

These cherubs gently flew,
Looking like rose-buds fresh when radiant with
      dew,
  And then there followed angel-men of song,
  Chosen for lovely voices from the throng
    Of singers who have passed
Out of the Abbey-choir into the Unknown Vast.

To them no stone was raised,
They had but lived, and sung, and died, and
      upward gazed
  For glory, when their duty on the Earth
  Should fructify into a nobler birth
    Beneath a lovelier sun,
And full of finest music to the Greatest One.

These angels in the nave
Clustered in silent wonder, while the vergers
      gave
  Each one a surplice, pure and lily-white,
  A robe most fitting for such sons of light,
    And then they walked in twos
Over the echoing pavement into the choir pews.

    There all the great had gone,
Summoned by some mute influence from their
      state forlorn
  Of thraldom in a museum of stone,
  As if for all our sins they did atone
    In icy silence drear,
Until Heaven's trump should sound and bid the
    dead appear.

    Then rose a priest and said :
" Ye chosen men of England, flowers of the dead,
  Here in the quiet breathing of the Night
  We are assembled to behold a sight
    More wonderful than thought
With finest mesh of fancy hath conceived and
    wrought."

    And then the altar blazed
With an effulgent glory till all eyes were dazed,

And from the picture on the altar-screen
There stepped the twelve apostles on the scene,
    In Eastern robes full dressed,
Ready to do their Great Redeemer's least behest.

    And o'er the altar bright,
Slowly receding, rose a far-extending light
    Upward through wall and roof to the blue sky,
    Connecting time with dim eternity,
      And down the vista flew
Our Saviour, with sad eyes that looked us through
    and through.

    He came as comes the morn,
In silence light diffusing o'er the Night forlorn,
    And though His glorious eyes looked soft and sad,
    One felt as though some day they would be glad
      When His great work was done
And goodness filled the heart of every earth-born
    son.

    And when great Purcell saw
This far-unfolding glory, he was filled with awe,
    And struck at once those chords which herald in
    That chorus of Christ's victory over sin,
      Which was from Handel wrung
When he the glorious life of the Messiah sung.

Loud Hallelujahs rose,
As crashed the harmonies' reverberating blows,
  'Gainst wall and roof in triumph o'er sin slain :
" For the Lord God Omnipotent doth reign,
    King of Kings, Lord of Lords,"
Was sounded up to heaven in high ascending
  chords.

Great Handel looked afraid
As Purcell this high honour to his music paid,
  But Purcell knew it was a master flight
  Of genius up the dizzy steps of light
    To thrones of burning gold,
Which all ascend with fear, however strong and
  bold.

And when the chorus ceased,
All eyes instinctive turned towards the burning
  East,
  Where shone the Lord before the altar fair,
  A halo streaming from His wavy hair,
    And as He raised His hand
We felt a mystic silence pass along the land.

But when we heard Him speak,
His wisdom for the strong, His comfort for the
  weak,

Our hearts were moved, just as a sea-borne breeze
In sultry summer makes the sun-burnt trees
    Lift up their branches high
In their delirious greetings to the light blue sky.

    It even seemed as though
The Gothic roof of sun-gilt palms waved to and fro
  In sympathy with the sweet song he sang,
  As his loved voice amongst their branches rang
    In plaintive accents clear,
And all our eyes were rainbow-hued with many a
    tear.

    " Why came this human breath
Out of the womb of travail to dissolve in death ?
  Why as a Man of Sorrows did I live
  To shed salt tears and all my labour give
    To lift men out of grief
Into the Heaven of purity and sweet relief

    " From conscience-pricking woe ?
Why have ye men of thought let all the centuries go
  In selfish longings after hills of Fame,
  With all the energies of life aflame
    In crushing brethren down,
That ye may get their slavish hands thy brows to
    crown ?

"These statues and these busts
Are largely monuments to thy o'erpowering lusts ;
  The Royal Henry who this fane did build,
  Now bears me witness that he was not filled
    With love for me alone,
But reared the Sacred Palace that he might
    atone

"For sins conceived in youth ;
As if he could with blocks of stone corrupt the
    Truth
  In Him who is the Truth and made the stones,
  And gave to Man his house of flesh and bones,
    But left his soul quite free
To carve his heart's design on Time and Destiny.

"Oh ! that ye had been wise
Ere ye had passed the Gates of Death, and then
    thine eyes
  Would have been ripe to bear the blaze of
    light
  Which, past those misty portals, met thy
    sight,
    And ye would then have been
More ready to discern those truths on earth un-
    seen.

" More quick to be impressed
With all the sweet refinements of the pure and blest,
More gentle and more kind, more high in tone,
Fine courtiers of Heaven near the Almighty
throne
Of all-inspiring Truth,
To which I drew the World with my own life for-
sooth.

" Ye who have passed thro' Death
Into the higher regions of Immortal breath,
Now know the mystery of human life,
And why its seething and continuous strife,
And why ye can but give
To God only the spirit of the life ye live.

" England remembers here
Her greatest, brightest children, and ye now ap-
pear
In one long line unfolding from the past,
And may it not be long before the last
Great heart shall seek this shrine,—
The full-developed being of the Light Divine.

" Taught by my grief and woe,
Men know now how to live and die, and what to
sow

To bear good fruit in the new life to be,
How germinating from their love to me
   Comes love to brethren dear ;
And yet how sad to see so little fruit appear.

   " Look now around, behold !
The man of luxury devouring his own gold ;
   See softly walking in the open air
   Hypocrisy, with a resentful stare,
     Cutting Love's tender heart
With his deluding aspect and performing part.

   " See how sweet Love doth die
O'ergrown with choking weeds of man's theology,
   Of which he gleans no more than what is writ
   In comprehensive Nature, though his wit
     He ever chides, to find
Some subtle theory to cheat his puzzled mind.

   " And thus he wastes his time
In puerile creeds and doctrines, while the life sub-
     lime
   I came to teach remaineth undiscerned,
   He thinks fine music, churches, incense burned,
     Confession to a priest,
A sordid money-offering, a holy feast,

" Will make the Lord forgive
The sins and selfish follies of the life men live,
  In which delusion Man will calmly die,
  To find a rude awakening on high,
      Where his unfitted soul
Still must be schooled in sorrow, till Love makes
      it whole.

  " Look at that master dread
Who grinds his helpless workmen till they starve
      for bread
  And cry aloud in pitiful despair
  From stifling dens of thraldom, till the air
      Is salted with their tears ;
Yet through that cry for mercy Love itself ap-
      pears.

  " Look at that servant, too,
Who scamps the daily work his master bids him do,
  And lives without a sympathizing thought
  For all the hazards that the times have brought
      To business far and wide,
While he floats sullenly upon its turbid tide.

  " There always will be poor,
And some will riches gain, at whose well-guarded
      door.

The poor will ever knock and beg for aid,
And bless'd is he who from his store has paid
    His guerdon to the cause
Of tender Love, the Mother of all righteous laws.

    " The poor and rich alike
Take sordid views of life ; it never seems to strike
    Their dull conceptions, they should live for
        those
Who teem around them buried deep in woes ;
    But ever they live on
Absorbed in sordid drudgery till their time has
    gone.

    " Yet progress has begun,
And the wise thought of England has a victory won
    O'er indolence, and poverty, and shame,
    By joining hand to hand in mutual aim
        To gather wealth from far,
So that her hills and plains with factories covered
    are.

    " Thus money-profits spread
From rich to poor, and he need seldom starve for
        bread
    Who can but work ; yet sloth will still com-
        plain,

And greed still wrack its ever cruel brain,
　　To turn the drops of sweat
Squeezed out of labour into gold to fill its net.

　　But some day man shall see
Through spectacles of Love, and poverty shall flee
　From out the land ; and then all men shall learn
　That Capital is Labour, and shall burn
　　In Love's contagious fire
All enmity and greed as a sin-funeral-pyre.

　" Would that I saw abroad
This spirit paramount, instead of flash of sword
　And sound of drum and herald trumpets blown,
　While every nation 'neath huge debts doth
　　groan,
　　In face of coming war,
Listening on lightest words of kings in solemn
　　awe.

　" Behold ! how race hates race
And nation envies nation, standing face to face,
　Armed for the fray, so that the living world
　Shall deluged be with blood and onward hurled
　　To anarchy and death,
Until those left alive may curse their very breath.

" England, beware and live !
Be strong, united, bold, yet ready to forgive,
  Hurl him from power who setteth class 'gainst
      class
  And race 'gainst race, and panders to the mass
      Of men who fain would steal
Their brothers' envied wealth, teaching their
      hearts to feel

  " It is their own by right,
(For he who boldly steals thy goods in the broad light,
  Though he announces all that will be done,
  Is none the less a thief whom men should shun) ;
      And I would have ye pierce
All moral farce and crooked thought with hatred
      fierce.

  " Are ye my Priests of Love
Who stand and scoff at one another ? Look
      above !
  Aim at the highest in your inner life,
  Slaughter not Love before my eyes in strife ;
      E'en devils can agree
In friendliest communion in their hate of me.

  " How can ye hope to gain
The victory o'er Death and sin if ye remain

For ever in your pulpits pounding forth
High-sounding doctrine with abusive wrath
    Against your fellow priest ?
Although not one can tell what comes when life has
    ceased.

    " Awake ! or ye will find
The man of thought and science leave ye far
    behind
  In the great struggle after truth and light
  In this wide sea of darkness, where the sight
    Is apt to blur and blind
The full expansive vision of immortal mind.

    " For ye must know I send
The spirit of my life with every heart to blend ;
  It present is at every human birth
  Of Christian or of heathen on the earth,
    And in full time shall kill
The vile hypocrisy that doth my kingdom fill.

    " It is not life to eat
And drink and sleep and breathe ; Life must be
    strong with heat
  Of Love, and climbing-thought and hope in-
    tense ;
  Man lives full conscious of some influence

Beyond his earth-born dreams,
Giving his soul a foretaste of Heaven's joyous
gleams.

" But sorrow shall be found
For ever on the earth, or how can Love abound ?
For Love awakened is by sympathy ;
Men cheat themselves who think this life can be
A paradise of bliss :
Man must be schooled by trials here, the Heaven
to kiss.

" Let then my Priests beware,
For they stand full before the world in Heaven's
bright glare,
The pioneers of the souls of men
Out of the darkness of this earthly glen
To regions high and fair,
Where Faith lives ever strong and fresh in purest
air.

" It will not ye avail
To lead the rich to heaven while all the poor bewail
Their tattered garments as unfit to blend
With dainty ladies who the Church attend :
Out to the hedgerows go !
Show men ye dearly love them in this world of woe.

" For Love is all that saves ;
It brought me to the Earth, goes with men
through their graves ;
And ye must ope your arms to all mankind,
Bring in the vile, dishonoured, deaf, and blind,
And bid the brutes awake,
Till Love shall move creation like an earthquake
shake.

" I authorize no creed
But Love, which makes true life ; by Love all men
are freed
From dismal depths of selfishness that cloud
The Light and cover with a misty shroud
The mirror of the mind,
Which should reflect the eye of God in all man-
kind.

" First, Love ; and then, the Light ;
Last, Home ; where man shall see his brother
chaste and bright,
Not wrapped in flesh which masks the inner
soul,
But heart revealed to heart, a perfect whole ;
Home, where I love to be,
Waiting to greet all hearts that long for Love and
me."

With this his sweet voice ceased,
And then he through the vista passed ; the Light
    increased
  As he receded from our view ; as though
  He wished to fill us with the lovely glow
    That from his Being came ;
And then the choir this carol sang with glad
    acclaim :—

LOVE ! LIGHT ! HOME !

  Love ! Love ! Love !
Floats on the flood-tide of tears,
Burneth through night-shades of fears,
Glistens when sunlight appears,
And dies not, worn out with the years,
  But blossoms, and ripens, and yields
  Fruit in Heaven's glad harvest fields.

  Light ! Light ! Light !
Comes like the passion of Spring,
Out-flies swift birds on the wing,
Riches eternal doth fling,
And asks none a payment to bring,
  But throws to us all a soft kiss,
  And lights up the pathway to bliss.

Home ! Home ! Home !
Dream of the prodigal's night,
Nestling so warm in the Light,
Where passion feeleth aright,
And brethren no more disunite,
But love in the Light and the Grace
That shines from Christ's sorrow-sweet face.

AN OUTCAST IN LONDON ON SUNDAY.

A MONOLOGUE.

I AM an outcast in these London streets :
    If I knew it not,
Soon would I find it written on men's faces
As they pass me by, and swerve away from me
    In morbid fear.
      Weak souls !
    They know no better,
They have not learnt the holy breathings
    Of the Son of Man !
      Learnt, I say,
    They *speak* Him glibly,
For His words are cant upon their tongues,
  But in their hearts they know Him not,
And ignorantly wound, and bruise and murder
    Him.

    Here on this Sabbeth morn
    Where is my Christian brother ?

Out midst the poor?
Striving to lift his fellows from the dust?
Kind-hearted, tender, true?
Alas! not so;
He stands before his mirror in his pride,
Leisurely lazy,
Decking his body o'er with gaudy robes
That foster envy in his neighbour's breast
At Sunday show,
And I am left to wander unbefriended.

Yet not so unbefriended,
For in these treeless streets
The sweet wind clings about me in its joy,
And blows me God's kind kisses from the skies:
Last night it must have slumbered upon beds of
flowers,
For in its balmy bosom I can smell
The incense of the violets,
Waved from their petal-censers by its
lulling arms,
Down in the mossy woodlands by the hyacinths.
Yes; I am not alone,
The Wind is still my friend,
For to my heart it bears
The whispering love of warm Humanity,
And when it kisses me,

Brings me the kisses of my brethren too,
    And fondles all alike.

    Ah ! my proud friends !
Christian, Mussulman, or vain Hindoo !
    Who claim to find salvation,
        We all are brothers,
        All are kissed by God,
And round us circulates His Mighty Wind,
        As 'twere His Spirit,
    Mixing our breaths together ;
And so you cannot stand apart from me
        E'en if you would ;
The wind destroys for ever all your thoughts of
      caste ;
    You cannot say,
" I will not have this breath of God about me,
That circulates amongst the common herd
      And touches me ! "
    For without breath you die.

In the sweet open air to rest at night
I've lain with Winter, while his icy breast
    Has chilled me to the bone :
I've slept with fickle Spring, and felt her breath
      Blow hot and cold with all her varying
    moods :

And wide awake with Summer through the night,
I've watched the spirits pass across the sky ;
    While, in sad Autumn's lap,
    I've dreamed of Life in Death,
As her ripe fruit came tumbling to the ground.

    Know you not, Oh ! Man !
    Lit with this Sabbath morn,
Here, in these quiet streets (where Mammon's wains
    Are silenced for a time
In grudging fear of the Almighty will),
That Labour cries for leisure more and more
In God's great name ?   That slaves are dying fast,
Replaced by freemen Mammon cannot bribe ?
    That *Life* is what we aim at,
    Not *bondage* to our brother,
But high attainment, help, and unity,
And all that's kernelled in that one word,—Love ?

If you loved your brother, would you thieve ?
Would you kill, or slander, or suppress him ?
Would you deceive him, and be jealous of him ?
Would you not take him kindly by the hand
    And bid him sing,
Rather than fancy you could sing the better ?
Oh ! to be jealous of a brother is too base for man !
It hides sweet Love as Night will veil the Day,

Breeds murder in the soul,
Acts like a torture in the heart,
Curdles the spirit like an acid stream
 Injected in the blood.

Know you that Christ is breathing in the millions
 As they toil in joy or sorrow,
 Though they know Him not?
That like a breeze He fans their upturned faces
  As they sweat with labour,
And in a mighty multitude press on to God?

Christ is far greater than His Church,
And mightier far than our small minds conceive
 Him;
 You cannot cramp the liberty of Love,
 You cannot lay down rules for it,
 And say, " My heart must go no further ";
You cannot rule it by a band of priests
  'Twixt four church walls;
 Man ever falters from his trust
  When sorely tempted,
 And what are priests but men
  Self-consecrated?
Then look not to the East or to the West
  For high salvation,
 But follow Christ's great spirit through the
world.

God 's prisoned in no creed,
　　But breathes in all,
And all must breathe in Him.

But I am prisoned in my flesh
　　For some wise end,
I feel to-day much as a devil feels
Prowling the Universe in search of plunder,
　　And realize how easy 'tis to fall
　　　　Into the Deep Abyss,
Further and further from the light of God,—
If it be possible to lose that light
　　Which permeates all.
　　This flesh I drag about
Is like a fettered weight that pins me down
　　And curbs my pride ;
What evil might I do, were I but free
　　From these tight body-shackles !
See this smug, demure, well-fed, and happy citizen,
Pacing his smart-frocked family to church
Without a thought of me, (except to sneer
At poverty and rags, and ne'er-do-weels
As though they were a plague). Were I but
　　free
To wander as a spirit, I would prick
His easy conscience and unlock his heart,
And torture him with such a tenderness

For all the poor, that he should never know
One quiet hour.
>Were I but free,
>Proud with imperfect knowledge,
I might be tempted to defy my Maker !
And so 'tis better far that I should fettered be
With this poor fleshly body, than unmoored
From Earth upon the Spirit-Sea, till God
Thinks fit to launch me.

I'll follow this too happy man to Church
And hear his doctrine ;
>" Too happy," did I say ?
Ah me ! would we but knew
What danger lies in too much happiness,
And what a safety-valve our sorrow is,
While we're encased in crusted selfishness !
Can any pearls compare in wealth
With the rich tears that spring in Sorrow's eye
>Out of sweet Love's distillery ?

>Too happy man !
Your soul is never swept by passion's wave,
Never exalted to Thought's mountain peaks,
Never transported to the clouds of heaven,
>And blown about in glory ;

But lies reposeful in the soft warm arms
   Of sensual bliss,
And sees no vision greater than itself !

Whither trend your footsteps, my too happy
  man ?
  What goes your soul to hear ?
  'And will your Church receive me ?
   These, my faded coat,
My linen worn to rags by ruthless soap,
No longer catch the favour of man's eye,
Though there is poetry in every fold
Of these old robes that riches cannot buy;
This well-worn suit has long ago been dyed
Deep in the essence of adversity,
And I am half inclined to feel more pride
In tatters than in new-made tailors' clothes ;
For garments gather round them old romance,
Old histories that none can truly read
But those who wear them. Let me then, O !
  World !
Remove the pity from your eye ; my pride
Rebels against it ; for whate'er I am
You have most surely made me. When I cast
With easy, gay, and mad indifference,
My patrimony to the cruel sharks
That haunt Society's sad, wreck-strewn sea,

I found no friend to save me, and here stand
Stripped of illusions on this Sabbath morn,
An Outcast, but a better, nobler man,
Schooled by your bitter lessons, scornful world.

  And now, too happy man,
Will your fine Church admit me ?
And may I sit beside you in your pew,
  As though I were your friend in tatters ?
Pray let me try your Christian charity :—
I will slip in between you and your Church
    And stop your progress,
And ask you whether you can find me room ;
  "No !" you say, " the pew-op'ner will grant a
    seat to me ! "
  And yet you have a place to spare !
  Shame, shame, upon your ice-cold heart !
Oh ! Lord ! canst Thou look down from Heaven
  On such a mean professor of Thy love,
And yet allow his shallow soul to breathe
    In Thy fair world ?

I will within, and see and hear once more
My brethren and my sisters pray and sing ;
The verger tells me he can find me room
In this great Sanctum Evangelical,
Where now no poor man strives to set his foot,

Awed by so much respectability !
Where pews are hired for money, and the rents
Swell out the Parson's purse, how can the poor
        Be welcome guests ?
The poor, so proud in their humility.

        Fling wide your Churches' doors,
You who would Christlike be !
        Why want you money,
        Downy beds and rest,
                You Priests of God ?
You, who by sweet Sorrow should be rent
        For all the sins of man.

Keep down, wild heart ! throw off all bitter
        thoughts,
Hear you not music in the air ? so pure,
So tender, so appealing, so sincere,
And yet withal so sweetly reas'nable ;
It seems to make the very air feel holy,
As though God's spirit hovers round the place
And gazes through the windows with soft
        eyes.
        Such music, wooing me,
Is like the dying soul of Summer
    Wooing cold Winter's breast
    In plaints of soft despair !

That organ note,
Deep delvèd from the bosom of the earth,
Rolls its soft thunder round my soul
And mingles with the melody that streams
In purest thought from Heaven !
There is no doctrine in this melody
To rend the mind,
And make the heart of man
Too small for its humanity ;
It circles round its " tonic " with delight,
Coquetting freely with its "dominant,"
And knows no other law.

Just as the unseen fingers of the storm
Sweep mystic music out of Nature's harp,
So feel I in this place, and I would breathe
The surging passion of my heart in song :—

Rouse me to fight
For the Good and the Right,
Oh ! Music of Trumpet and Drum !
Pulse through my blood
With thy magical thud
As I march for the glory to come.

Lull me to rest
On the throb of thy breast,
Oh ! music of Pathos and Pain !
Thy throb may beat time
To the tenderest rhyme
That ever sobbed through a sad brain.

Let my heart dream
On thy melody's stream
Oh ! music of Rapture and Love !
Or let me float
On thy loveliest note
To the ears that are listening above.

Let my feet bound
To thy metrical sound
Oh ! music of Dancing and Joy !
Then will I chase
Time's marks from my face
With the ease of a light-hearted boy.

And in the gloom
Of my bodily doom
Oh ! music of mystical Death !
Let me arise
Like a bird to the skies
On the wings of my vanishing breath.

K

" Does God in very deed dwell on the Earth ?
  Behold ! the Heaven
And Heaven of Heavens cannot contain Thee,
  How much less this house
  That I have builded ? "

  Thus spoke a mighty soul
Out of the mists of dim antiquity ;
Music was then a baby wailing tunes
  Upon its treble pipe,
Unconscious of the magic power that dwelt
In dormant chords and discords
  In its tiny breast.
Had Solomon but heard these liquid tones
Poured, like a stream of honey, from this organ's
   throat,
  He would have cried in fear,
  " This is the voice of God,
Beseeching, calling, all our hearts to Him."

  But Music, after all,
Is but the passion of the soul,
  It only sings us God,
  And goes no further,
  Just as the rose exhales
The perfumed breath of the Almighty,
  And gives us nothing more.

Now long I for the words of thoughtful Man ;
Man, with his mighty faculty of reason ;
　　His glory in himself ;
His boundless, restless, deep imagination ;
Surely his inner sense can see, and feel, and
　　know,
The sweet communion of a Spirit-God
　　In the deep silence of his soul ?
　　Man ! the inheritor of all the ages,
A greater teacher than the birds or flowers,
　　Or magic music thrills !

The voice of Music dies upon the air,
And in an awful hush the priest proclaims
　　His views of God :
　　Alas ! the pigmy that he rears !
Born of the earth-bound tendencies of Man,
　　The gift of sensual ages,
　　When Cain, the tiller of the ground,
　　The gardener, the man who loved the flowers,—
And must have had soft pity in his soul,—
　　Grew wrath with Shepherd Abel,
And, God-defiant, sacrificed his brother
　　To jealousy and riot of the heart,
　　And dull, black-hearted Murder !
　　So Christ, the priest now says,
　　Was but a sacrificial Lamb,

A slaughtered innocent to God's great wrath,
    Who could not, till the Spotless Lamb was
      slain,
    Forgive His erring creatures ;
But now, the sacrifice complete, we all may come
    In Christ's good name,
    And find supreme salvation,
Or die for ever in the lowest Hell !

    Oh ! murderous priest !
Bloodthirsty preacher of God's tender love !
How can you hope to draw poor souls to Him
    In trustfulness and truth
    On such a base conception ?
    'Tis true Christ died
    (You even wound Him now),
Yet Man it was who crucified and pierced Him,
And drove Him, guiltless, to that cruel grave,
From whence have started all the flowers that
    grow :
    Pansies for Ease of Heart, the Rose for Love,
    Daisies for Innocence, and Hawthorn's eager
      eyes for Hope.
    God in His mercy-seat
    Sat pierced with pain,
    All wrath with His creation ;
He put His hand upon the sun

And hid the light,
He shook the earth
And made men fear and tremble,
While Christ's great spirit floated back to Him
Upon the wings of Love,—new-born.

New-born !
Ah ! Yes ! until that Death
The world knew naught of Love !
But then men learnt the joy of melted hearts,
The holiness of sorrow,
And the brotherhood of pain !
Christ died for all, 'tis true,
That all might live ;
But *that*, most shallow priest,
Is vastly different to your bloody creed,
Your brutal lowering of the God of Love !

God, the Creator, is no murderer,
And wants no murder to appease His wrath,
Like an Almighty Cain ;
I must away from here,
It warps, confines, reduces, and suppresses me !

Oh ! the glad air !
The laughing sun !

The blessed wind !
The boundless blue !
The freedom of elastic thought again !

The churches fill as tho' with clustering bees !
So many hives, and yet such dearth of honey !
As if there could be famine in the land of Love !
Here is a church whose humble front
Entices me ;
The verger, lolling at the door,
Laughs when I ask him why he's not within,
And says, his work is done,
'Tis now the parson's turn !
Proud is he of his parson,—
A great magician in the realm of thought,—
Whom men come miles to hear :
Who long since coffined all his superstitious creeds,
And sang grand Unitarian litanies o'er their
grave,
Blowing his fame abroad.
No Mother Church should ever cramp him down,
Or hide his vanities beneath her robe,
He would, 'fore all, rebel !

And there he stands,
Reading his Sunday essay of neat word-mosaics
To all his worshippers ;

As useless as a brass-band in a wilderness
    For rousing souls ;
  Is this the fire of Truth ?
This the persuasive passion of the heart,
The magic inspiration on the lips of one
Who comes from close communion with his God ?
  He speaks of Goodness, Truth, and Beauty,
    Love and Art,
And plumes himself upon his bright-eyed Reason,
  Jeers at a Resurrection, scorns a Miracle,
  Laughs at an Incarnation,
 Yet has the graciousness to think
That God still liveth in the heart of Man !

Oh ! Pride ! thou self-inflated one !
Twin sister of weak, blind-eyed, self-conceit !
  How canst thou venture in these holy places,
    And talk thine impotence ?
  There is a time when Wisdom cries for silence
    And whispers to the heart deep mysteries.
  God, the Unthinkable to mortal minds,
    Can surely be Incarnate if He will,
    Can work new wonders,
    And can sport with Death,
Without rebelling 'gainst His Mighty Self ?

We ill could spare the tender Mystery
That made a sinless Son to save the world,
  Lit up the Cross of Love on Calvary,
And shone new wonder through the eyes of
     Death.

       It stirs the heart,
    It makes the pulses beat,
It sends sweet music murmuring thro' the air,
It makes us hear the beating heart of God,
  And feel the rush of Love in all mankind ;
    Call it a superstition if you will,
       Pale academic mind !
    Still shall it charm my days :
Yea ;—though I scorn their brutal thought of
     God,—
'Twere better to be washed in Christ's warm blood,
  In Sanctum Evangelical,
Than to be chilled in Unitarian ice,
Borne from the Polar regions of humanity.

    I'll leave you to your icy dreams,
      Pale-minded Priest,
  And seek elsewhere salvation,
That all the storm-tossed billows of the mind
      May be at rest ;
  Good-bye ! thou fleshly verger,

Lolling against the pillars of the porch,
No wonder thou dost love the open air,
  The sun, the breeze,
  The buoyancy of Nature,
And turn'st thy back upon the artificial ice
  That's made within !

I, who have sought my bed beside the blushing fox
  gloves
  'Neath the brambles,
 Or by the blue-bells in the dell,
Or 'neath the wild-rose tangled in fair Summer's
  hair,
  Know something of the Love that paints with
  joy
 Its story on the earth,
And pipes its love-songs through the tuneful
  throats
  Of merry birds,
Yet feel I something lovelier far
  Lives in our hearts
And longs for utterance upon a harp in Heaven.

  What heart can speak it here ?
  Who would believe the tale ?
  To tell a man you loved him fondly
  As you might love a woman,

Would make his heart recoil !
For here our minds are like a garden rare
   Locked against all intruders,
That none may see the lovely flowers that bloom,
Or taste the fruits that ripen 'neath Earth's sun.

As I have lain beneath my woodland coverlets,—
   And watched the action of the kindly clouds
Sponging the tear-drops from the weeping moon
   To strain them on the earth,—
      Oft have I felt
   That I could weep and die
In deep despair at man's unfriendliness.

   I'll leave this city-wilderness of souls,
   And hasten to the laughing woods and fields
     To read God's Bible there ;
For man seems destined to confine his soul
     Within his prison walls,
   A captive to his terrifying flesh,
A martyr to the social bonds that bind
The tongue from speaking what it finds
Deep in the silence of the inner man.

Now I ascend the mountain of the Lord
   Where all the air is pure.

Come to me here, ye hard of heart,
Ye bitter, biting souls of malice born,
Here on this peak where Summer pins her
    gown
And drapes it gracefully adown the land.
See how it crinkles in the grassy vales
In thousand tints of green, and gold, and brown,
And how the fine embroidery of flowers
Is woven in its texture like a dream,
How the wild poppies flood it deep with red,
And large-eyed corn-flowers star it o'er with blue,
And how the cattle trample on the dress
Unheedful of its dainty loveliness,
Bellowing their music to the tell-tale wind
In joy of grassy feasts and sunlit hours ;
And see that river weeping thro' the vale
Bearing Earth's sorrow to the distant sea.

Tell me, ye hard of heart, if ye can breathe
In these rare altitudes, and watch the sun
Lay his fair bosom on the breast of Night
Without some thought of God, some glimpse
    divine
Of glory throbbing in the distant blue,
Some fascinating feeling that o'ercomes
The fleshly sense, and bids us float away
Into the Silence, far removed from care ?

Whence comes this feeling, this strange, soaring
    power,
As I stand dreaming forth into the west
Verged on this precipice ?   And whence the cry,—
"Cast thyself down ! " while my poor body shrinks
From the weird verge in dread and cries ;—
    "Tempt not the Lord, thy God,
Who made me as a casket for thy jewel-mind
To hide in, till the Day shall come
When flesh shall gravitate and soul shall soar."

Pass, coward thought !   I cannot break the spell
    Of my existence,
For if I throw the casket o'er th' abyss
    And shatter it,
Still will the jewel-mind exist,
Tho' nebulous it may hereafter shine
    Amid Heaven's diamonds.

He must be coward great who craves Oblivion
    And longs for Nothingness,
Like a whipped felon conscious of his crimes !
  As well expect the wind to be quiescent,
    The sea a glassy mirror,
The clouds fixed monuments upon the sky,
    A's to conceive that Man
With all his possibilities can die !

Life ! Life ! Life !
Reels like a dance before me ;
Death through all Nature merely means a change.
And now will I rest happy on this peak,
Till the rich beauty of the sleeping heavens,—
A velveted arcade of soft, aërial blue,
In silent Midnight wrapt—
Forgets its glory in the Eye of Day.

Look ! as I gaze the Love-light flickers round
    me,
I see it flush the hill-tops with soft gold
And flood the sky-line with Aurora-bloom ;
I watch it modestly peep into valleys,
 To chase the miasmatic fogs away;
And Man, awake to righteousness,
Brings his pure heart before me,
That I may read him without doubt or fear !
    No more concealment !
But perfect intercourse from mind to mind.

All hail ! thou Light of Love !
    For Thee
The sky-lark bears Earth's morning song to
      Heaven,
In palpitating haste to pierce the blue ;
The thrush sings anthems to the waking woods,

While Morning stands on tiptoe, holds her breath,
And spreads a mystic hush along the land,
That all may hear the passion of the song,
And Man at last may see, and hear, and know
All the sweet things enfolded Love in Thee.

This surely must be some great Day of Days !
I see a coffin laid along the valley,
And men and women packing it with lies
Which they have hugged as life-long, fond
        delusions ;
I see the Pope throw in Infallibility,
His Priests, their scorn of fatherhood,
The Turk, his Woman-Heaven,
The Buddhist, his dead-thought Nirvana,
The Calvinist, his living Hell,
The Miser, all his suffocating greed,
The Thief, his silent cunning,
The Hypocrite, his false devotion,
The Monk, the stupid torture of his flesh,
The Slanderer, his bitter epithets,
The Flirt, the base deception of her eyes,
All things that war against fair Truth and Nature,
And then in one vast funeral
They twine along the valley to the sea,
    And there beneath the waves,
Bury this coffin packed with Life's great lies.

And Love reigns over all ;
No brother now left desolate ;
No sister left to wander out her grief ;
No mother famishing for bread ;
No heart left yearning for the eyes of Love,—
(Lulling its passion with some drug that grew
When Summer, drowsy with her own great heat,
Swooned in the arms of Sleep ;)
No dreary poverty where beauty dies ;
No rich-man's treadmill in the jail of Time ;
But all, in happy helpfulness to one another,
Losing the doom of Self
And gaining Life's great heritage of Joy,—
Like seedlings bursting through the earth
To show their beauties to the wooing sun.

And look how they come flocking to the side
Of this unworthy Outcast !
Fain would they draw me from my brooding self
Into the blessed freedom of their love,
And fain would I go with them,
To be once more free as air.

Oh ! Love ! thou sunlight picture of the heart of
God !
I feel thee in my soul,
And as the world goes moving to the West,

(Where lies the Great Hereafter
　　Wrapt in the sunset-clouds,)
My heart gleans something of the light to come ;
The barriers of my Mind are blown away
　　By the great Wind of God,
And far-unfolding visions meet my gaze,
Like those fair pictures the balloonist views
　　As Heavenward he flies ;
This Earth is but one small revolving speck
　　As through the Air I pass
　　　　Into the Ether,
Upwards, ever upwards,
To the Fatherhood of All.

SPIRIT REVELATIONS.

*Thoughts unsealed by the contemplation of Nature and
my own complex Being.*

THE sea has bowed its white-capped waves to me,
  The clouds have beckoned me to yon deep sky,
The sun has drawn me with its wondrous heat,
  The wind caressed me as it passed me by,
And flowers have looked in pity at my face,
  And butterflies tossed past me in disdain,
While trees have whispered through their shivering
    leaves,
  And birds have talked to me of joy and pain ;
Yet have I been a fool and noticed naught
Of all these miracles that have been wrought.

And they have been so gentle and so kind,
  So patient with me, as if I were great,
And they but lowly things upon the earth,
  Their only pleasure on my soul to wait.
How long the wheat has borne its ears for me,
  And waved them to me on a sunny day,

With silky ribbons rustling in the breeze,—
  The fruitful chemistry of common clay ;
Yet have I passed them by as nothing worth,
And never loved these sweet things of the earth.

I've seen the mussels cluster round the rocks,
  To lay their belts of blue upon the grey ;
I've seen the limpets' tiny pyramids,
  Tint with prevailing brown the sea-girt bay ;
I've watched the ivy clambering round a wall,
  To paint its tottering masonry with green,
And in the furnace of the sinking sun
  What gorgeous colour-pictures have I seen !
Yet though I've seen, my inner sense was blind,
And never ope'd the windows of the mind.

And I have heard the babbling brooklet sing
  A mystic cadence as it ebbed away,
And listened to the birds high carolling,
  When they were taking summer holiday ;
And I have heard the roar of cataracts,
  And mail-clad grasshoppers' one-noted song,
And awe-struck 'neath a Heaven robed in black,
  I've heard the awful thunder boom along :
Yet have I hearing, heard not in my heart,
But deaf remained to all this wondrous art.

And I have smelt Spring's distillations sweet
  From violets, hyacinths, and cowslips pale,
Lilacs and Maybuds ; and on summer nights,
  When woods are hushed to hear the nightingale,
I've breathed the breath of star-aspiring pines,
  Carnations, heliotropes, and roses red,
With trailing honeysuckles' o'er-sweet breath,
  Breezed through the window as I lay in bed :
Yet all these scents mysteriously distilled,
Have with no wonder my dull being filled.

But now I'm looking for the subtle sense
  That underlies these wonders ; for the hand
So light, that made those evanescent clouds
  And poised them graciously above the land,
As sun-blinds or rain-carriers of heaven,
  And ever-changing pictures of the skies ;
For Him Who gave the sun eternal heat
  To make these clouds from earth-bound vapours
    rise,
Who made all colour, scent, and sound,
And wrote in rocks the history of the ground.

And from within me comes a quiet voice
  Vibrating to the harmonies around,
Telling of Joy and Sorrow, Love and Hate,
  And all fine secrets that in hearts are found :
The delicate perception of the Mind,

The varied feelings that our beings fill,
The longing for perfection, never neared,
    The Hope undying and the magic Will ;
And I, a wonder to myself, do cry
To some High Fatherhood in Earth or Sky.

And I shall find Him ; for it cannot be
    That I may feel affinity and still
Have no real kinship with the Father Mind
    Who works these wonders with His Mighty Will,
The Painter, Poet, Stone-historian,
    And great Mechanic of unmeasured Time,
Who uplifts mountains and controls the seas,
    Whose simplest structure is a work sublime,
Who has a willing choir in every grove,
Composing Anthems to the Lord they love.

'Twere shame to look the morning in the face
    With eyes impure, or gaze with vile intent
On spotless maidenhood ; and how can I
    Approach the Maker of the Firmament
With eyes that have no thought of reverence,
    Forgetful of th' Almighty Breath of Morn,
That stirred the world to life and gave us hope
    Of unveiled wonders at a Second Dawn,
Which shall upon us break through mists of Death
When Earth at last doth covet us our breath ?

We try to peer into the Spirit Land
   With sensuous eyes, forgetful that ideas
Are spirit-born and come from some High Source
   Unseen : we cannot even *see* our fears,
But *feel* them burning with electric force
   Into our being ; and it e'en may be
That what we witness with material eyes,
   May be but figments in immensity,
And all that's real is our encagèd Mind
Groping in this dark Earth with vision blind.

Oh ! seas and woods ! 'mid magic of starlight !
   Oh ! sun-born flowers, grassy hills and vales !
Forgive me for my slighting thought of you
   Who are so *real* to me. Oh ! nightingales !
Recall me to the Earth I love, and sing
   To me your lullabies of Night again ;
Lament in melody your hearts' regret
   At my vain treason, if it give you pain ;
Woo me with music, and invite the flowers
To yield their secrets in the sunny hours.

But no : you beauty-loving earth-born eyes,
   You ears that ravished are with tender tone,
Why cramp me with your narrow range of power,
   When I to spirit-land allegiance own ?
Our bodies are the trial of our life,
   Our home of sad temptation, where we sigh.

But as a seedling doth evolve its shell,
  So life within me was not born to die,
And I for ever must a spirit be,
Full of expansion in futurity.

Earth is but an instructive toy for man;
  The nurse who nurtures him upon her breast,
And bids him fathom out the Secret Mind
  Which lives in all things, without sleep or rest.
The flowers tell us of some tender care,
  And seas and mountains utter forth wild praise.
On nights of starry wonder when the heavens
  Are cleansed from every cloud, we upward gaze
And lose ourselves in dim infinity,
Conceiving something of what yet may be ;

But when Heaven's nearest star, Earth's golden
    sun,
  Doth shine upon the wealth of wood and stream,
Day steals the diamonds from the velvet sky,
  And brushes out our night-bejewelled dream ;
Our minds are lured by sense from high desire ;
  The present hides the future and the past ;
That which is near obstructs our larger view ;
  But when we find Him in the future vast,
Earth will have faded from our sensuous eyes
And Higher Thoughts have borne us to the skies.

MY HEART'S LOVE-TRAGEDY.

THAT breath of wind which shivered through the
    trees,
Said something strangely sweet to my rapt ears :
         You heard it not ?
         Why should you ?
       To you 'twas but a breeze
        That came and went,
To me it whispered music from the long-past years.

Could ever Love be sweeter, more divinely born
         Than ours ?
Did ever Love give promise of more joy ?
When, like the opening of the buds of flowers,
Or like the influence of the rising morn,
It drew the secrets from our silent hearts.
Oh ! Love ! thou wondrous vision of Eternal Truth,
       Clad in Eternal Youth,
       Thou arrow-armèd boy !

The trees were whispering then as they are whis-
    pering now,
And twilight mystically clothed the green

In robes of softened beauty 'gainst the sunset sky;
I saw a gnarlèd bough
Plunged in a bath of purple,
Look like a giant whose whole life had been
Spent in some silent combat with the powers on high.

The sun seemed loth to close his tired eyes,
Tho' worn with his hot gaze at Mother Earth,
As in the west he lay,
Seeming to slumber in some gorgeous dream
That died out at its birth,
In fitful gleam.

All things seemed clad in velvet, soft and weird,
And dark were all the vistas 'neath the trees :
I almost feared
I saw a fairy 'neath a bed of fern
Combing her tresses by the glow-worm's light.
But what one sees
When over-weighed with thought on such a night,
Might make a dead man start and turn
Ere he was ripe for resurrection flight.

They say the dead do rest in peace,
(God grant they do) ;
But have you never seen

How tumbled lie their graves in churchyards old,
As tho' their pent-up bodies struggled for release
    From consecrated mould
And tottering tomb-stones long since choked with
    green !
(Time fain would heal our griefs and dry our tears,
Would e'en unwrite the records of sad years.)
    They say some dead have broken through,
    And walk the world in miserable plight,
    Clad in transparent sheets of mystic white,
Dumb, pantomimic spectres, who their past do rue !

Was it a ghost I saw on that fair eve,
    Walking with such mute ease ?
'Twas clad in white and made my bosom heave
    Fond thrills my heart did seize,
    My brain did fancies weave
      As on it came,
I saw it kill my fairy 'neath its feet,
And quench unheedingly the glow-worm's light ;
    I felt a throbbing heat,
    Th' approach out of the night
Of something that would light my love in never
    dying flame.

    It was no ghost :
    It was a fairy who thus killed a fairy,

And did unconscious murder on the threshold of
    my love,
      Portents do come to most,
      E'en to the Godless and unwary.
      But I had no belief in charm or fancy,
And treated them as idle necromancy.

      A bat flew out !—
    Blind chance would have it so ;—
      It fluttered round my head,
      And put the moths to rout,
      Then darted with a cruel blow
At that white form as on it sped.

The clammy touch of that foreboding bird,
The shrink of horror from that blow unseen,
The creeping dread that froze the pulsing blood,
      Unnerved that figure white ;
    No sound the woodlands heard,
      Nothing disturbed the scene,
But life was checked when in its full-tide flood,
And swooned away limp from its magic might.

      To instant help I rushed
As that white figure slid upon the ground,
I tore the clothing from its jealous clasp,
      While all the earth was hushed,
      And there I trembling found
A woman swooning in my frightened grasp.

I thank the Lord that all the air was dim
With shadows from the half-drawn veil of Night ;
    The crescent moon with its keen, glittering rim
        And one bright star,
        Shed not sufficient light,
But chastely hid her bosom from my sight,
That I might dream of what her beauties are.

The air felt stifling 'neath the heavy-coated trees,
    And so I folded her within my breast
(Which ne'er before had such soft beauty pressed),
    And bore her helpless to some grassy plot,
        Where stole the fitful breeze,
And the blue eye of Heaven looked calmly down,
Weeping cool tears on Earth's dry, sun-scorched
        gown.

        There was a pool close by,
      All stagnant, recking, weed-encircled ! . . .
    How could I sprinkle such vile drops on her
        Who looked so pure ? . . .
      At last I heard a sigh
    Long-drawn ; life was returning :
    And like a vain idolater,
        With wild soul burning
        In forest fane obscure,
I knelt ecstatic ; holy love discerning !

There in the dusk I saw the eyelids lift
And two wild stars peep out,
As if new-born and full of fears ;
Lode-stars they were in my love-firmament.
Storm-clouds might drift,
Whispering friends might warn,
And venomed tongues might shout,
But I was bound just like those Eastern seers,
To seek that Bethlehem where my love was born.

Born in the breezes of a summer night,
As tho' sweet angels rustling 'mid the leaves,
Drew us together,
Or pleasant devils wrapt me in a charm
Of warm love-weather,
And lured me with that vision bright
Of two fair arms all lily-white,
Peeping out coyly from their silken sleeves.

I cannot tell
Until the Latter-Day,—
When this wild Earth as incense to the Lord
Shall burn, and waft our spirits far away
Up to the footstool of the Judgment Throne,—
Whether the influence came from Heaven or Hell ;
But this I know,
That Love can never die, however lightly sown,
And being born of God, He cannot Love disown.

I lifted up my sweet one from her bed of leaves
        and grass,
And led her gently forward lest the briars might
        hurt her feet,
    And she, still faint and cold,
   Kept murmuring her thanks ; while I, more
        bold,
   Would not permit such thoughts her lips to
        pass,
For was it not itself reward to tend on one so
        sweet ?

At length her coyish diffidence fled like a cloud
        away,
We skipped from chill December to the summery
        month of May,
   And from her lily throat there came
    That voice which thrilled in me
The sympathetic chord of Love for all eternity.

" My heart leaps up to you, kind Sir, with mad,
        wild, fluttering throbs,
   I pray you pardon my impulsiveness ;
      Pity my sobs ;
   Had you a magnet 'neath the forest trees,
   To draw me onward to your resting place
      Beside that bed of fern ?

You ne'er, I trow, will guess
Why my sad soul, so quick to faint and freeze,
And creep within itself, trembled to meet you face
to face,
When that strange bird came dashing 'gainst
my brain,
Like some weird harbinger of coming pain.

" Think me not lonesome, like that pine forlorn,—
A leafless sentinel upon a wind-swept hill,—
For I have friends, though I seem unbefriended ;
Your new mind comes to me like rain from
heaven
Upon the dainty Earth,
When surfeited with too much wooing of the
amorous sun ;
I would my life had blended
(As God gave it birth),
In the high aspirations of a greater one.

" But I am bounded by a mindless zone,
And know that mentally I live alone,
So on fair summer nights I wander thus,
To hold communion with my friends the trees
And list to the communicable breeze."

I heard this speech with wonder ; can you doubt
  My strange affection now for Nature's words,
When whispered by the softly sighing wind
    Amid the leaf-clad branches ?
    I could not live without
These fine remembrances of other years,
When Nature poured her tale into the listening
    ears
Of that sweet woman's high-aspiring mind.

We came then to a tree uprooted in some long-past
    thunderstorm,
  And stretched all lifeless on its Mother's breast—
    Sad as a woman dandling her dead babe—
    There sat we till the crescent moon
      Sank in the glowing West,
    With all the world aswoon
      In midnight rest.

  And there we talked ; she told me how her life
    Lay buried in the quiet of a farm,
  How the once-cultured garden of her mind,
    Walled round from harm,
  . Now grew but weeds and brambles,
And was a weary wilderness, without a charm.

"I now am chained," she said, "unto a churlish
        lord
Who has no sort of mind above a clod,
        Who cannot speak a cultured word
            And knows not God !
My parents chained me to him for his gold,
        And were I ne'er so bold,
        I cannot break the law-locked chain,
But must this churl's sad wife for aye remain."

Then said she, starting up with merry bound,—
"To-night, howe'er, I'm free ; free of his hateful
        arms,
For he is to some break-neck hunting gone,
        And I have no alarms ;
Here will I spend the night, if you with me will
        stay,
And with a wise philosophy chase time away."

And I was nothing loth, for I was but a man,
        And she the daintiest woman Eve had ever
            borne,
            Dainty in word and thought,
                Dainty e'en in scorn,
        Yea, no such dainty creature, since the world
            began,
                E'er smiled upon the morn.

I lay outstretched on that old trunk, how long, I
    cannot say,
She dallying round me in her playful, winning way,
    And as I skyward peered, I thought I saw
Blue veils from Heaven fall draping round my couch
    Bedecked with tearful stars—
    Like costly curtains with no woven flaw ;—
And then I felt the curtain lift, and 'twixt the sky
    and me,
Two radiant eyes and two sweet lips appear,
Which gently dropped on mine, light as the falling
    dew,
Then froze with fear and suddenly withdrew.

A kiss may have no meaning, or epitomize a life,
    May be the breath of innocence or lustful shame :
But *that* kiss came to me as Earth attracts the rain,
    As skyward springs to life the burning flame,
As rivers ever wander to the thirsty sea,
Drawn by the never-failing law—Necessity.

Come down, ye moral ice-hills from your scornful
    heights,
    Melt in love valleys, twine thro' glens of roses,
Then with new sympathies and new delights,
    Touched with the sorrow the warm world dis-
    closes,

M

Try and condemn that one, that only kiss,
And from High Heaven, the angels pure would
hiss.

I know how passion surged within me as those lips
came down,
How near Love's chariot whirled us to th' abyss !
You ! with your granite heart ! may sneer and
frown
At this my " sentimental bliss,"
(I see you sneering now),
But know that critics have been rarely born
Who can discreetly scorn
And yet attain
A wealth of wisdom and a crownèd brow.

After that kiss I knew that all had changed,
For I had lived, like you, amid a frosted world,
Which had no feeling for a soul of summer,
Amid negations had my spirit ranged,
I wrapped my soul in heavy funeral pall
And walked beside it, like a sorry mummer.

And so that kiss, though nectar to my lips,
Frightened my coffined soul,
Like poison-sips,

And for one minute, dazed with treacherous doubt
　I gazed all dreamily about,
And watched her silhouette against the sky
　Melt in the secret wood ;
　Then like a wakened chrysalis
　My soul burst thro' its bonds,
　And, armed with new-born wings,
Flew through the woodland's dreamy shadowings.

　　But she was gone :
　　The darkness held her tight
　　In its weird grasp,
　　And now my heart forlorn,
　　Waiteth ;
Till in some western sea before the setting sun,
A ship with her loved form shall float to me,
And we shall sail together out into the Night.

SERMONS IN NATURE.

" THE bells ring out in merry jingle,
　And high and low together mingle,
　　Flocking to church :
　The shop-girl dons her best attire
　And daintily avoids the mire,
　　On goodly search.

" Shall I aspire to such devotion ?
　Or join the grand song of the ocean,
　　Hymning God's praise ?
　Or can no thought of mine be holy
　Unless I trust my being wholly
　　To priestly ways ?

" Can any temple be erected
　In which God's love can be detected
　　Without their aid ?
　Am I not undivine and human ?
　And must I not be made a new man
　　Or be unmade ?

" Alas ! alas ! I know no better,
  I'm Nature's child without a fetter,
    Knowing no care ;
My Priest, the ever restless ocean,
  Waves incense by perpetual motion,
    Free as the air.

" And all ye crushed in shrines and churches,
  Leave to false priests their self-made perches,
    Envy them not ;
They'll soon be lean with scanty feeding,
And careless of their Heavenly breeding,
    Lament their lot."

          So passed a stranger
Torturing the listening air with these tumultuous
    breathings ;
  Had he sound philosophy ? truth ? yearnings after
    right ?
Or were his wild convulsions only peevish teethings
Essential to the product of the tooth of wisdom
  Which only Time can ripen ? " Where's the
    Light ? where's the Light ? "
And he received for answer only dim discernings
  Of underlying good beneath the crust of fashion :
Nature like a fire seemed to quicken all his yearn-
    ings,

And cramping human customs only roused his
    passion ;
Men seemed so much alike in clothes and mode of
    thinking,
No one could be unorthodox and hold his station,
While ever-changeful Nature kept his Faith from
    sinking,
And made him feel her God-song was no vain
    oblation.

So through the fields he went,
    Perfumed with breath of summer ;
The bells' high jangle wildly rent
    By hurrying wind made changeful murmur,
Till cresting o'er a fir-crowned hill,
    Wind, bell, and insect-music blended
In the wild thunder of the sea,
    With quaintest harmonies attended.
A band of unseen minstrels gently
    Followed his steps and sang and played,
Streaming abroad melodious plenty,
    For.which no money may be paid ;
And when his brain and ears were flooded
    With all these heaven-descended lays,
His heart imprompt with words unstudied,
    Bounded to God in Hymns of Praise :—

" Oh, wind ! I thought you rude and coarse
 Years back ; I missed your hidden meaning,
The sea was boisterously hoarse,
 A veil my vision intervening,
Which the forgiving wind in wonder
 Has tossed into the boiling sea,
And now I welcome Nature's thunder
 And join your hymn with childlike glee.
Welcome, ye groves, and vales, and mountains !
 Welcome, ye cataracts and streams !
Welcome, ye heaven-sprung crystal fountains !
 Welcome, ye golden sunlight beams !
Welcome, ye sentinels of ages,
 Worn by perpetual duty bare,
Old rocks round which Time frets and rages,
 Sun-crowned with beauty, towering there !
Welcome, thrice welcome, sunlit ocean !
 Tossing in foam each new-born wave,
Glad in thy free, inconstant motion,
 Which sleep ne'er dares to make its slave ;
Carry my song round all the globe-lands,
 Tell men to breathe, and live, and glow,
Tell them the trees are angel robe-stands
 Beneath Heaven's blue-arched portico,—
Decked now with hangings star-bespangled,
 And now with moonlit fleecy clouds
All prism-tinted and entangled,

And fading fast like ghostly shrouds,—
Tell them the angels soft as sunlight
  Come in the Spring when Nature's bare,
Weave wood-anemones and violets,
  Primroses and cowslips rare.
Tell them the birds sing songs far purer
  Than ever mortal lips can sing,
No law for them makes Death the surer,
  Or ever arms him with a sting ;
But turreted in leafy chambers,
  Shaded from mid-day's burning rays,
And garlanded with Spring-tide blossoms
  Foreshadowing fruit in Autumn days,
They sing their love-songs and their dirges,—
  For they have joys and sorrows too,—
Unconscious of the guilt that urges
  Us sinful men our lives to rue.
To them our God is no enigma,
  They love Him, breathe Him, every hour,
Knowing the bounty of His Mercy
  Is ten-fold greater than His Power.
Did not our Saviour pray in secret,
  Soul-fed by moonlight's watchful ray,
With tears of star-land falling o'er Him,
  When human hearts were far away ?
O ! all ye men dried up in form-life,
  Worshipping ugly-shapen creeds,

Prepared by priestcraft for your thraldom,
   Regardless of your crying needs !
Here there are sermons writ in Nature,
   Unspoken epics from the skies,
Symphonic chorals of creation,
   Refuting atheistic lies !
Come then and worship God in beauty,
   God in the Spring-unfolding trees,
But come with childlike, wondering faces,
   And fall entranced upon your knees."

MY FORMER SELF.

ALL withered seem the branches of the tree of
 Thought
  Which has grown up within me ;
Oh ! for the fire of prayer
To burn the dead wood in a flame to Heaven,
And waft my spirit to the Great Unseen !

Broken away from half my father's faith,
  And faint with floods of tears,
   Pity me, Lord ;
Lend me Thine aid ; restore those branches fair,
Which waved their sacred incense in the winnow-
 ing wind
  In years gone by;
For surely 'twould be kinder to preserve
The shady influence of that sheltering tree,
Where thoughts grew happy in Arcadian bliss,
Than let its dry wood perish in despair of Spring
  And give no grateful shade.

Nay ! Nay !
The change has come,
The electric fire of Truth
Has struck the tree,
And burnt away its green serenity ;
And now I know
That roses may into sweet lilacs bloom,
And daisies blossom into daffodils,
And Heaven lose its canopy of stars,
Sooner than I can turn into my former self.

My former self is dead !
Slain by the new-born man within me ;
Each new thought, like a javelin,
Pierced and pained him,
And left him bleeding in the march of life,
And now men call me cruel,
Fratricidal,
And point the finger with a look of scorn
As though forsooth *I* were a murderer,
And *they* the pillars of immortal Truth.

They are the murderers, not *I !*
Their pulpits ofttimes are but scaffolds where they
slaughter Truth,
And plague the Sabbath with mere lip-beliefs !
Vain hypocrites !

They worship long-dead creeds
To which they have not given decent funeral ;
    They mouth sweet prayers unmeaningly ;
    They shout anathemas to frowning Heaven,
And clutch at silent shadows when they die !

        Yet Truth will live ;
    A lying thought has no recurrent Spring,
        But dies for ever,
    While Truth ne'er knows a Winter ;
        And so my former self
Lies buried in the vastness of Life's dream.

    And now I find it sweet to talk with Death
    And let him lead me to the Border Land
        Where spirits rest,
    To that star-studded gate of blue
    Which hides the Eternal Silence.

        Perish Corruption !
        Live, New Life !
    And show me where God dwells,
In violets, lilies, roses, fruits, and seeds,
In magic mountain-peaks preserved in snow,
In chasms rent by angry Mother Earth,
In valleys melting in soft luxury,

In rivers, lakes, and seas,
In moon, and sun, and stars,
 And Heaven's soft blue ;
And closer in the bleeding heart of Man,
In tenderness, in pity, and in love,
 In spirit-gleams,
 In hopes and fears,
And in the wailings of the weeping years.

 New Life ! grow bold,
Knock loud at Heaven's great heart
 And wait for Joy.

DENIALS AND REFUSALS.

OUR lives are moulded by each day's denials,
And purified in furnaces of trials ;
    So long as we are *sensitive* and *feel*,
Then are we sure of high perfection ;
    But if our callous hearts soon heal,
We may reap Heaven's rejection.

Life's building-stones are made of great refusals ;
So love we not our inner-life's perusals,
But hide them from the gaze of all our fellows,
Altho' we trumpet forth our praise with well-
      worked bellows !

      See how the child aspires
      To satisfy its innocent desires,
      But how each day it learns
      To quench the fire that burns,
Growing well-cultured with its heart in hand,
Ready at any moment to expand

'Neath mad temptation,
In an unbounded fury of elation ;
But in the end suppressed,
It lullabies to rest.

See how the lover knocketh at a heart
            To find no answer,
Yet like a bounding hart,
            Or furious prancer,
He runs the faster after his endeavour,
From which no obstacles his soul shall sever ;
His cold refusal makes him twice a man
Intent upon his plan,—   .
And yet the fates would tell him that his bliss
Will never linger in a grudging kiss,—
Away with bars and bolts ! no heart's protected
When once the majesty of Love's rejected !

And watch, too, how the worldly man aspires
            To storm Society's fortress,
And how the jealous world up-fires,
            With Pride as portress,
To hinder his admission,—
For curs must never hope to live with dogs of high
        position !

And yet the more he is refused,
The fuller is his blood infused
　　With mad determination,
Until at last he turns the lock
And proud as any strutting cock
　　Forgets his former station.
Refusals feed the appetite
　　Of every man's ambition,
And spur him in the social fight
　　To better his condition.

And note, too, how the man of thought
　　Inspires weak words with meanings,
When with fine passion he has caught
　　Life's intellectual gleanings !
And how his treasured words with glee,
Full of his soul's immensity,
He pours into our listening ears,
Regardless of our laughs and jeers ;
He who would cleave the Heavens and weigh a
　　　　star,
Who sees th' Almighty from afar,
Can trample on our futile sneers,
Can mount above us far away
To regions of eternal Day !
The more his teachings are refused,
The more his dreamings are abused,

The higher his unbounded flight
From the drear regions of our Night,
Until in time he lifts us higher,
Near his volcano peaks of fire !

Come then, most sweet Denials !
Come then, my darling Trials !
And with thee I will build a palace fair
Whose minarets shall gleam in Heaven's bright
  air.

THOUGHTS.

HAVE thoughts no habitation ?   Do they grow
   Like fungus in a night only to wither ?
Or does their spontaneity surely show
   They come from spirit-land and we go thither ?
So strangely evanescent !   Who can tell ?
   They may be but the shadow of a lie
      And we as well,
   But, if so, surely 'twould be well to die
      Ere we come hither !

Have thoughts no habitation ?   How they flit
   Like fleecy vapour o'er a summer sky,
Leaving no stain to mark the course they quit,
   Having to earth a born antipathy,
      Like globes of gas
   Borne on the mighty breath of Boreas.

Suppose that great Photographer—the Sun,
   Pictured our thoughts upon the Heavens above,
      Would it be well ?
   Would Hate turn into Love,
      Or Heaven to Hell ?

THE BOOK OF SIN.

A Dream.

Fain would I wander in eternal Spring,
   Ere the hot sunbeams scorch the tender leaves,
When thrushes teach their nestlings how to sing,
   And swallows build their homes 'neath dewy eaves,
     Then, late in glorious May,
Fair is the earth, and green, and ever gay !

To breathe the breath of lilies in the vales,—
   Where violets blue their tell-tale blushes hide
From the wan lover who, despairing, fails
   To find those scented offerings for his bride,—
     Is like inspiring breath
That wafts the soul beyond the realms of Death.

Then bright-eyed primroses in moss-grown glades,
   Shine gaily forth, like stars in clustering bands,
And light-blue hyacinths, in dewy shades,
   Deluge with incense all the forest lands,
     Then apple-buds flush bloom,
And may buds fill the hedges with perfume.

And then it was that I first found my love,
  The fairest blossom of a golden year,
A flower for whom the bluest skies above
  Distilled the choicest dew-drops—sweet and clear,
    A rose of sacred birth
Offered by gracious heaven to me on earth.

And I accepted her with joy most meet,
  No heart with richer offering could be blest,
I prayed to God that I might give my sweet
  All that the land could render of the best,
    That when Death came to me,
Our love might blossom in eternity.

And full of love one sunny afternoon
  While gentle breezes fanned our souls to sleep,
And May was merging into lovelier June,
  A wondrous vision did my senses steep
    In ecstasy sublime,
Like dream of prophets in the olden time.

High in the sky great flocks of wild-birds flew,
  While in the West a blood-red sunset blazed,
And mighty trees in a great wind that blew,
  Were violently uprooted as I gazed,
    Then a dead silence came,
More awful than the wind or Western flame.

And then a sudden blackness quenched the light,
  The sun had fallen, stifling grew the air,
Owls shrieked and vultures screamed in wild affright,
  And made me tremble in a vain despair,
      Then thundering earthquake shocks
Shattered the houses and the mightiest rocks !

And then the awful stillness came again ;
  I peered for help into the blackened gloom,
But saw not, heard not, and like one insane,
  Rushed frantically forward to my doom,
      And in the darkness fell
O'er a steep precipice that led to Hell.

Stunned, wounded, broken with that maddened
        plunge,
  I lay, and found the dismal gloom had cleared,
And prayed that some kind spirit would expunge
  From my shocked vision the dread doom I feared,
      As on a ledge I lay
Afraid to gaze below or crawl away.

Then like a glimpse of Spring in Winter bleak,
  A lady, sweeter than a new moss-rose,
Came down to help me with demeanour meek,
  And vowed to love me e'en till life should close
      And we should give up earth
For the grand issues of our heavenly birth.

Her words, so warm, sank in my wounded heart,
    And soothed me like the scented breath of morn,
I pointed downward and I saw her start,
    I told her I'd ne'er loved since I was born,
        And then she raised her eyes
And spoke her feelings in a glad surprise :—

" I come to lead your thoughts to dwell on me,
    Lest they for ever wander in unrest,
Flitting from flower to flower gay and free,
    A butterfly existence, never blest ;
        Lover of beauty find
In me, a helpful and a loving mind."

And in that twilight dim my soul had found
    The love that had been haunting me through life.
I took her hand and o'er the tangled ground
    And jutting rocks that cut us like a knife
        We climbed the dreadful steep
And o'er Hell's brink resolved our love to keep.

Then like a frightened fawn to me she clung
    As with a crash the sky was rent in twain,
And through the gap a gilded Book was flung
    Towards burning Hell : but with a cry of pain
        An angel like a dart
Flew down and caught the Book to his wild heart,

And settled on that ledge where I had lain,
  Reading with greedy eyes the Book of Sin,
Forgetful that the heavens had closed again
  And he no more could free admittance win ;
      Sin bound him in its spell,
And in a thunder-bolt he reeled to Hell.

I asked that gentle lady by my side,
  Why to the angel she no succour gave ?
She could not tell ; her sympathies were wide,
  And yet she felt her mission was to save
      But one, her love, her sweet,
Who with a gentle kiss she now would greet.

And with that kiss I woke ; my lover's eyes
  Had watched my moving features as I slept
And wondering at my passion-breathing sighs,
  Suspected I some secret slyly kept ;
      At this I raised my head,
Then softly told my dream and weeping, fled.

Fled with the weight of thought the dream had left,
  With no interpreter to help or guide ;
Like one who when of all his friends bereft,
  Seeketh in some lone nook his head to hide ;
      Yet felt I Love had been
Breathing its influence in that dreamland scene.

SENSUALITY OR LOVE?

Canst thou tell me, Heaven,—
Decked with thy crescent moon and wondering
      stars,
Watching for ever the appealing Earth
In all its futile struggles with old Time,—
Why my flesh yearns for those two lips and eyes
Glowing with passion's flame, as in their gaze
Mine own melt helpless in entrancèd bliss?
So that I fain would kiss my life away.
Or canst thou tell me, Spirit of the World,
Thou iron-hearted daughter of stiff Pride,
And sister of Hypocrisy and Death?
Or Nature with thy wondrous chemistry,
Who know'st the secret colouring of flowers,
And paintest with deft hand the sunset clouds,
Canst thou explain the working of my soul?—
The mortal consciousness that dies Immortal
In the receiving bosom of the Great Unknown?
For here am I with eyes turned Heavenward,
Bent towards high purpose and exalted thought,

Plunged on a sudden in a bath of passion
Brimful of sensual joy.

    Flesh tells me it is Love,
But Mirror Conscience cuts me like a knife,—
As though its glass had broken in my heart,—
And shows me flesh doth lie ; the lips are sweet,
The eyes seem incarnations of the soul,
But spirit doth not answer spirit : Love doth sleep.

What art thou, O Love ? Honey-dew of the soul ?
Manna in this heart-wilderness ? a breath ?
A beam of light, a substance, or a dream ?

    Come to me, Love :
Let not a simulating thing betray thee,
And rob me of the sacred joy of knowing one
Who has so precious been to all mankind.

THE SPIRIT OF LOVE IN THE SCENT
OF THE HAY.

BUTTERCUP-GILDED grass! first offering of the
      Spring,
  Suffused with sorrel red, tinted with bells of blue,
Can I forget thy sweetly scented breath,
Thy perfumed incense at the shrine of Death,
         In early June?
       Shall I not rather sing
  All that my heart unfolds in love of you?

When you were dying fast, embalmed in odours
      sweet,
  I on your bosom lay, sunshaded by green trees,
Thinking of nothing but the joy of rest,—
The ecstasy of langour giving zest
         To my repose,—
       When, lo! two pretty feet
  Came stepping towards me with a careless ease.

Those pretty peeping feet with rustling music
　　came,
　I looked with shyest glance upon the lovely sight,
And stealthily peered upward to her face,
Adorned with golden hair and broidered lace
　　　　And healthful bloom ;
　　　My heart was all aflame,
　Cupid's rash dart had pierced me in its flight.

Feigning myself asleep, I watched her drawing
　　near,
　Her cheeks all lily-white and then a blushful red ;
Love, wildly palpitating, startling guest,
Stirring tumultuous music in my breast,
　　　　Had pierced hers too ;
　　　And I could clearly hear
　Our hearts beat time together as she said :—

" Mystic approach of Love, borne on the breath of
　　Spring,
　Bird-winged omnipotence, panting within my
　　heart,
Move this loved form, embosomed in sweet hay,
With thrilling heart throbs nothing shall allay,
　　　　But my true love !
　　　Lend me thy dove-like wings,
　That I may kiss his cheek and skyward dart."

Then as she, queen-like, stooped,—Oh ! do not
    coldly frown,
  How could I shun that sweet temptation of my
    life ?—
She blushed her heart into her velvet cheeks,
I kissed like one who hidden treasure seeks,
        And scorns delay ;
      I showed her how Love's crown
Would aid me like a charm in life's hard strife ;

How all my high ambitions would now bud and
    grow,
  How, merged with her sweet nature, mine would
    turn to gold,
How men would learn to love me for her sake,
And strive, by helping me, more smooth to make
        Her course on earth,
      And how to them we'd show
The path of light to Heaven, ere we grew old.

I drew the rosy picture with such subtle art,
  That, at the sight, she melted into sunny tears,
More sweet to me than all the laughter bright,
Which she would scatter round from morn to night,
        Like light for all ;
      For me alone her heart
Welled up in tearful joy and drowned my fears.

We made ourselves rich presents on that day of
     days,
  Worth more than all the gifts we buy with golden
     store,
For we ourselves to one another gave,
And promised, with sweet oaths, to be the slave
       Of each to each,
     To share both blame and praise,
  And knit our souls together more and more.

NANCY'S TRYSTING AT STAPLE INN.

TRITE BUT HUMAN.

Recited by her when an old lady.

I WAS a girl of seventeen summers,
Oh ! such summers !
The sky and the land and the sea
Were a Paradise to me,
And I was the same to all comers.

I had not a thought of a Fancy,
Tiresome Fancy !
To me a boy was a boy,
And a man a too-heavy toy,
Tho' they called me their charming Nancy.

I went fast asleep in the moonlight,
Lovelorn moonlight !
I had but to lay down my head
On my little poppied bed,
And my senses were lost till the noonlight.

But my ever sweet, watchful mother,
Forgive me, Mother !
Came in the morn to my side
And opened my eyelids wide,
Lest the poppies of sleep might me smother.

I was a girl of sixteen winters,
     Oh ! such winters !
   I revelled in frost and snow,
   And liked the wind to blow
Till it tore the tree-branches to splinters.

(Blow gently now, Northernmost breezes,
     Horrible breezes !
   An old lady's limbs cannot bear
   Rough usage in the rude air,
And my lungs are all full of sad wheezes.)

How well I remember that morning,
     Heavenly morning !
   When the summer was hanging its head
   As it drew near its wintry bed
To sleep numbed in the cold till next dawning.

In the crowds of the streets I was walking,
     Thoughtlessly walking !
   I was looking at Staple Inn,
   Which the new world was trying to win
While the artists were futilely talking

Of old-world traditions and beauties,
     Quaint old beauties !
   Which we must not allow to be touched
   Or sacrilegiously clutched
By the Spirit of Change in its duties.

I walked in that charming quadrangle,
  Old, old quadrangle !
  With its central tree looking so sweet
  In its wide encircling seat,
Which jealous new Progress would mangle.

I saw not a man standing near me,
  Oh ! too near me !
  As my mind wandered back to old times
  Picturesque, true ; but the crimes
Made me think if I lived then, I'd fear me.

But now in this age of advancement,
  Too quick advancement !
  I thought I had nothing to fear,
  And knew not my tempter was near,
Or that I would be prone to entrancement.

He was a man of forty summers,
  Cold, cold summers !
  But he had broad shoulders, and stood
  Looking at me so simple and good ;—
Was *he* quite the same to all comers?

For he took off his hat to me gently,
  Oh ! so gently !
  And he handed to me my own purse,—
  The keeping of which was my curse,—
Then he stroked his moustache indolently.

And I was a simple young creature,
     Too young a creature !
    And I thanked him with only a look,
    Which I fear me he sadly mistook
(As we can be betrayed by a feature) ;

For he broke into voluble talking,
     Oh ! such talking !
    And the end of it all came to this,
    That he'd ask me to grant him a kiss
If I came there next day when out walking.

And I left him with such a wild yearning,
     Torture of yearning !
    A volcano had burst in my heart,
    Flooding fire into every part,
There was nothing but scorching and burning.

Yet he was forty and I seventeen,
     Soft seventeen !
    And I was just budding with Spring,
    While he was in full flowering,
Long past the summer of loving, I ween.

The full-moon was shining that night-time,
     Soft sweet Night-time !
    In a dream I went to my bed,
    And pillowed my lovelorn head,
But I lay wide-awake till the light-time.

I looked at my eyes the next morning,
    Sweet love-morning !
    And they had such a far-away gaze,
    As though they looked thro' a warm haze,
Or a dream that had come as a warning.

My heart was all tender with dreaming,
    Soft, sweet dreaming !
    I could not define what I felt,
    Though I thought as a sweet I might melt
In the full cup of Love I saw gleaming.

And my mother looked tenderly through me,
    Too far through me !
    She knew that strange look in my eyes,
    To her it was no new surprise,
But she never betrayed that she knew me.

I was just like an innocent flower,
    Poor frail flower !
    I might perish in winter cold,
    Or blush and be sweetly bold
If the sun of love shone on my bower.

And the sun shone most bright on that trysting,
    Old, young trysting !
    The heavens were a clear velvet blue,
    Swept clean by white clouds as they flew
Through the soft summer air unresisting.

I entered that quaint-looking gateway
      Old, sweet gateway !
    And all nervous I walked to the seat,
    Looking modestly down at my feet,
Quite unlike good Queen Bess in her state-way.

I sat facing that picturesque portal,
      Charmed Love-portal !
    I knew none could enter that square
    Without seeing me sitting there,—
Oh ! my heart beat too quick for a mortal.

At my back sat a man full of laughter,
      Mad, mad laughter !
    He was charmed by a comic old man,
    Who through his life's history ran,
With no thought of what might come hereafter.

And I was amused at their sallies,
      Men's mad sallies !
    I ought to have gone from the spot,
    For I knew my dear mother would not
Have allowed me to list to their rallies.

I could not myself see their faces,
      Funful faces !
But I dared not look round lest I missed,
    The being I fain would have kissed
And fondled with loving embraces.

At length I grew very sad-hearted,
    Cold, dull-hearted !
  I had watched for his steps for an hour,
  While Hope died away like a flower,
And I felt half my life had departed.

Then the old man limped up for his dinner,
    Useless dinner !
  His companion then slowly arose,
  And who should his person disclose
But the man who had been my heart's winner.

He came close to me placidly smiling,
    Vain, vain smiling !
  I just gave him the tip of my glove,
  For frivolity never can love,
And to maidens 'tis rarely beguiling.

Oh ! why did I love with such fever,
    Love's sweet fever !
  A heart with no human thud,
  And with treachery in the blood,
Giving life to a subtle deceiver?

I know now Spring's true full-blown Fancy,
    Midsummer Fancy !
  Would not wait in that indolent way
  For a Spring-blossom fairily gay :—
But it *was* a wise lesson for Nancy.

MY IDOL SHATTERED.

My idol is shattered ;
It had not a heart ;
And naught would have mattered,
Except for that smart
Which Cupid, all mischievous, made with his dart.

It said it had feeling,
And very fine sense
Of honour ; so kneeling
In rapture intense,
I thought I might share in its glory immense.

It had wondrous beauty,
It e'en might have cried,
Give love and grave duty
To me as your bride ;
And I would most willingly for it have died.

I thought it had passion ;
   It raged, and it formed
Hot words in wild fashion ;
   But 'twas Vanity stormed,
And not the fine elements Love would have
   warmed.

It seemed to be tender,
   It had such soft looks,
It dressed in such splendour
   And read such fine books,
And loved to look charming in drawing-room
   nooks.

It glanced in all glasses,
   And touched its fair hair,
And ogled the asses
   Who sighed with despair ;
It turned on one side with a " Come if you dare."

But now it is shattered ;
   Its tricks are all dead ;
Its beauty bespattered ;
   Its glory all fled ;
And never again could that thing turn my head.

THE GROWTH OF LOVE.

OUR love grew like a quiet flower
    That's planted by the wind unseen,—
You press aside a leafy bower
    And there it blossoms 'mid the green.

There is no credit on my side,
    For all men love her instantly ;
The wonder is that such a bride
    Should give herself to such as me.

Hearts oft 'gainst one another bruise
    Like ripening fruit upon a tree,
And by the sudden contact lose
    Their hopes of love in misery.

But we but touched and forth there sprung
    A sweet communion into life,
Which will not cease when Death hath rung
    The Knell which bids us quit this strife.

SUNSET AND DEATH.

Out in the glowing West I watched the sun
    Sink like a molten orb,
  With its ruddy gold-light flashing
    Fiery beams upon the fleecy clouds
Floating in splendour in the azure sky ;
I felt that God dwelt in their wealth of colours
    No hand could paint,
    No tongue could e'er describe,
While angels wove them into patterns rare,
To drape the throne of Heaven, where all the
        blest
    Cluster like stars eternal.

The trees were bathed in soft ethereal hues
    Of mystic purple and translucent blue,
And all the earth was wonderful and lovely,
    Dipped in the sun's rich fount of gold
    As it hovered above the world.

But every passing zephyr seemed to whisper,
    " Dying ; "
  And the faint light of the evening star
Told that the colours were fading away,
Till myriads shining in the blue of Heaven,
      Hurried the waning twilight
        Into the distant West,
And threw the pall of night,
Deep-dyed in dismal shadows,
      O'er the fair eye of day.

  So Death comes on man ;
Sometimes as gently as the quiet day
      Melts in the quiet night ;
Sometimes as swiftly as the storm-clouds
        Rush o'er the heavens
      After the sun has set,
With the loud boom of distant rolling thunder
      Borne on the night-wind's blast !

A BANKRUPT'S LAMENTATION.

A MELANCHOLY eve ! light clouds with dubious
    gladness
  Rushing in hasty fear across a leaden sky,
And biting blasts of wind full of malicious mad-
    ness,
  Chasing the withered leaves tumultuously
    by ;—
As though some fiend unseen did all the elements
    defy.

Awhile ago the Spring had trustingly come
    hither,
  Lured by the breezes warm, borne from some
    southern clime,
And now the hedgerows green, in grief are fain
    to wither,
  Lamenting their sad lot, cast in such treacher-
    ous time ;
Ah me ! to see Spring's dress of flowers dragged in
    the Winter rime.

Adown the bay the sea doth rage and surge and
    quiver,
  Froth-foaming in its wrath, giving dire aid to
    Death,
And ships disarmed of strength ride in their
    chains and shiver,
  While sailors thank the Lord with their half-
    pious breath,
That 'gainst the harbour-wall the sea its fury
    scattereth.

The rain upon my face beats hard with constant
    stinging,
  I glory in the storm hurled at me from the
    clouds,
The wind howls by my ears, a song of ruin
    singing,
  And I, a ruined man, far off from human
    crowds,
Delight to see how Heaven its Love in devastation
    shrouds.

But can it be that I with heart once young and
    tender,
  Dandled upon the idle lap of luxury sweet,
Shall in a moment's time all the past good
    surrender,

All that I've loved of life, all friends I loved to
    meet,
Only because my pride is stung and lies dead at
    my feet?

Bankrupt and ruined now, how can I bear the
    stigma?
    Long had my utmost skill floated a painted
        wreck,
Until that gold-scare came, searching my great
    enigma,
    Asking the captain for gold—payment of a
        cheque
Which no financial tricks could meet, and so I left
    the deck.

And here I am alone, defying this wild weather,
    Watching the swift destruction of the budding
        Spring
With which my heart agrees, Spring-time and I
    together
    Shorn of our prospects bright, feel now the
        bitter sting
Of trusting to the hard, cold world our life's fresh
    offering.

Pitiless blows the blast, whirling in wild com-
    motion ;
  Pitiless grows my heart, mercy has left its
    seat ;
When shall I ever quench this fiendish-like
    emotion ?
  Which scorns all thoughts of good, burns with
    revengeful heat,
Against the cool stare of the world, now bitter,
    once so sweet.

Surely in all the earth no heart has so much
    sorrow,
  No mind is more disturbed with bitterness and
    grief !
A mist hangs o'er my path, clouding each new
    to-morrow,
  Winds whisper in my ear,—" Poison will bring
    relief ! "—
And shall I sinking leave to rot my life's unripened
    sheaf ?

They say, God guides the storm ; why, then, this
    mad destruction,
  Hailstones and clouds of gloom, lightning and
    thunder wild ?
What if He rules my heart and for some wise
    instruction

Tears up my former life, tainted when as a
child
I thought the false world's teaching true ? but now
I am reviled,

I see with new-born eyes and find some glint of
meaning
In all this wind and gloom, this surging of the
waves,
This turmoil of my heart : Ah ! yes, I'm swiftly
gleaning
Truth labyrinthed in storm ; we are our own
life's slaves,
And need be broken from our bonds or gain un-
fruitful graves.

My past life opens up : I see allurements bounding
Before the charmed gaze of my youth, those
ecstasies of sin
Which did my heart entrance, shorn of its moral
grounding ;
Will-of-the-wisps I chased, cobwebs I chose to
spin,
And now, so late in my swift days, naught but the
storm I win.

But hark ! that dirge of grief the wind is wildly
    flinging,
  Using its gusty breath in lamentations drear,
Doth falter down the hill ; soft songs of pity
    singing ;
  It gently skims the waves, inspiring no more
    fear,
The storms of Nature and my heart are spent,—the
    sky is clear.

MY LOVE'S DEPARTURE.

EVANISHING 'mid steam and smoke,
　　The steel-steed tore my love away,
Regretful farewells from us broke,
　　And yet I dared not bid her stay.

To bid her stay meant too much joy,
　　Too much of exquisite delight,
E'en now no arts that I employ
　　Can ever charm her from my sight.

I kept my tender feelings still,
　　Choked like a river near its weirs,
Pent up in placid depths until
　　They burst in cataracts of tears.

You cannot dam Love's current deep,
　　It must for ever onward roll,
No bonds can e'er in durance keep
　　The love that flows from soul to soul.

I conjure up my Love's sweet face,
   As on that morn she left my gaze
And pressed me in a wild embrace
   With pretty looks and winning ways,

And wonder whether we shall meet
   In happiness and peace again,
Or if as pass the moments fleet,
   Our lives shall severed be in twain.

In all my thoughts she lives with me,
   And sheds fresh hopes on my desires,
I would that all the world could see
   The aspirations she inspires.

Yet sometimes in my moments weak,
   I fancy she may not be true,
That all the love her tongue may speak
   May be but words :—Would that I knew

And so I find relief in prayer,
   And ask that God, who loves us all,
May grant us both His special care
   Who hears His creatures when they call.

SONG.—HEART-LONGING.

THERE is no sweeter charm to the heart that is
    longing
  For love and devotion from one it holds dear,
Than to watch the warm colours dissolve in the
    twilight,
  As the sun sinks to rest on Night's purple-dyed bier.

For I know how my Love rose in flames like the
    sunlight,
  And how it still burns in my passion-scorched
    breast ;
I would e'en like the sun sink away in Love-glory,
  And lulled in the chill arms of Night seek my rest.

Oh ! why was I torn with this mighty emotion ?
  This deep, tender longing for one I hold dear ?
But who blind to my passion scorns all my devotion,
  And will not be melted at sight of a tear.

The river must find out its way to the ocean,
  The earth must eternally roll round the sun,
And so shall Love's great heart yet throb that cold
    bosom :
  I wait and I long till we two are made one.

MY LOVE AND I ARE ONE.

My Love and I are One :
The trees through which the breezes play,—
  The tossing sea which laves the land,—
  Are but the work of one Great Hand,
    Greater than star or Sun ;
    And He it was who made sweet Love
  Play on our heart-strings like the breeze,
    Or rather like the tide of Ocean,
    With a wonder-stirring motion ;
  And now I sing with heart at ease,
    My Love and I are One.

A NIGHTMARE.

The full-eyed moon, rimming a coal-black cloud,
    Shone like a spectre on the night,
Then slipped behind the shroud,
    A buried light,
But suddenly peeped out again
And vanished, like an eye in pain.

The air was wild, and blew the rain about,
    Gustily furious as in wrath,
And brought full many a shout
    Hoarse from the North,
As if its lungs were old, and wheezed
With laboured motion as it breezed.

My wife and I sat silent side by side,
    Drawn by a fiery jet-black steed,
Which shook with fright and shied
    At headlong speed,
Tilting against the unseen wind,
As though some phantom spurred behind.

The steed would crane its neck to us in fear,
    Though tight I held the straining reins,
And sparks would then appear
    Along the chains,
Flashed from its great electric eyes
Like light which from a meteor flies.

We sped along a narrow country road
    Bordered by hedges, fully dressed
With 'broidered leaves and snowed
    With white flowers blest ;—
For Summer with a grace divine
On country hedge-rows seems to shine.

Imagination lit the lovely sight
    Of sunny flowers held in Summer's hand,
Hid while the skirts of Night
    Palled o'er the land,
And on the fury of the blast,
We smelt their secrets as we passed.

Never have mortals seen a sight more weird
    As through that flowered lane we flew,
For a silk dress appeared
    And hid our view,
Then dashed against our faces pale
With all the fury of the gale.

It smothered us ; our breath we could not get
    Until we tore the clinging wrap,
Heavy with reeking wet
    And murdering flap,
Out of our mouths, and tossed it far
Into the dark,—where spirits are.

The steed sped faster still, with terror rent
    To see the mystic wraith appear,
As o'er its head it went
    Flapping its ear,
Sending a shiver through its heart
More painful than an arrow-dart.

My gentle wife crept closer to my side,
    And through the gusts I heard her shout :—
" The darkness could not hide,
    The moon shone out,
'Twas sister Hetty's skirt of gray,—
The Night hides something from the Day."

My spirit crept along my nerves in dread,—
    For well I knew the mystic sight
Meant portent of the dead
    Haunting the Night,—
When out the moon shone purple-red,
And on the earth great blood-drops shed.

Then felt we that some murder cried aloud
    For vengeance to the tear-stained sky,
Cov'ring with dusky shroud
    That blood-red eye ;
The air's wild shoutings 'round our ears
Expressed intensely Nature's fears.

LOVE ENNOBLED BY SORROW.

Love in a lap of roses lay,
　　Letting the days go idly by,
Without the shadow of a care
　　Or echo of a sigh,
For Love said :—" What have I to fear ?
　　The sea is mine, the land, the trees,
And all things for my joy exist,
　　So live I in luxurious ease."

But storms of sorrow came at last,
　　And Love's fair eyes were dimmed with
　　　　tears,
And care crept wrinkling o'er his cheeks,
　　And sighs relieved his trembling fears,
And Love said :—"What, Lord, have I done,
　　That I should suffer all this woe,
That from my over-burdened heart
　　These welling tears should overflow ?"

And one night Love did answer get,
    Flashed from the star-eyes of the Lord :—
" Thy joyous heart was chastened sore,
    That it might pour its love abroad ;
For perfect love is sorrow-born,
    And mighty hearts from trouble wrought
Shall soar to heights unknown to those
    Who never set the World at naught."

TO LOVE.

Oh! Love! thou Star of Hope, yet distant far,
  How shall I ever reach thine inner sense,
  Thy heart of sympathy? a joy intense
It were to watch thee kindling from a Star,—
A steel, white point in heaven, whose beauties are
  Too cold for earth,—into a near, immense,
  Warm sun of Love; I would not then from
      hence
Wish to depart, but on a funeral car
Would pile my dead ambitions for the grave,
  And bask content in thine intensity
Of Life and Joy; Self would no longer rave
  Its dirge of vanity, for it would be
Dissolved in sweetest Mercy, born to save
  The weeping multitudes that know not Thee.

LOST FRIENDS.

When but a dreaming lad, I loved a boy
Around whose form my being strove to cling
Like a wild tendril.   As a rose enshrined
In that boy's bower of love, my heart enlarged
And grew in power and beauty ; but he fled
Into the darkness, leaving me forlorn.
And later came a maiden sweet to me,
Whose mind was like the blue unclouded sky,
And at the magic of whose gentle touch
I melted into loving ecstasy ;
But she fled out into the dismal night,
Tearing my heart-strings as she went her way.
But ere she left me, in my arms she placed
A pledge of tender love,—a human bud,
Flesh of my flesh, compelling homage due,
Lisping its wisdom words of innocence,
And playing with the days as they went by
But he fled out into the darkness drear,
As though he shunned my dull society
And sought his mother's in the wistful sky.

Ah! whither have you fled, you loves of earth?
I look in vain for any sign of you,
But yet I know your hearts must live again,
For well I feel my own life cannot die,
It breathes the breath of an immortal song,
And still will flutter forth into the blue
Singing its triumph like a sky-lark free.

A WOMAN'S LOVE SONG.

TELL me what doth most attract thee?
    Woman full of knowledge golden,
Burning Wisdom, found by delving
    Deep within the ages olden?
Or a sweet and simple maiden
    Coyly dallying with her shyness,
Full of sentiment unspoken,
    Free from all the Old World dryness?
                Answer me!

Or a nymph endowed with beauty,
    Hair resplendent, eyes all brightness,
Tripping o'er the graves of sorrow
    With a most unfeeling lightness?
Or a damsel decked with dresses
    Of the daintiest flitting fancies,
Shedding all her soul in planning
    How to catch admiring glances?
                Answer me!

For I long to be thine idol
   And would learn what thou would'st cherish
That two idols may be melted
   In one Faith, too strong to perish,
Love-Faith! Life's triumphant glory!
   God-born, deep, sublime emotion,
Soaring to the height of Heaven
   With a never-tired Devotion :
            Wilt thou then not answer me !

DESPONDENCY.

My heart seems weighted with dim sense of woe
    Impalpable,—but real ;
  I feel a lurid light is vaguely shed
  Upon the future looming far ahead,
While I in dread of an impending blow,
    Shrink from the sight it offers to reveal.

And yet I know the sky and all the trees
    Are full of strange, sweet song :
  Shall life no longer lure my heart to sing
  And be atune with every breathing thing,
While leaves may whisper to the kissing breeze
    And thrushes fond their evening hymns pro-
      long ?

Can that deep love that in my heart hath crept
    Be but a transient gleam ?
  Can gorgeous sunsets and the rose's scent,
  And those charmed green-nooks where our hearts
      have blent,
Lose their sweet influence and be swiftly swept
    Out of remembrance, like a vanished dream?

I cannot tell ; the strings of my drear heart
    Seem swept by fingers weird
  Into alternate discord and wild dirge,—
  Like cries of drowning 'mid a boiling surge,—
And I seem drifting more and more apart
    From all the friends who once to me adhered.

Daisies are timorous of the darkening gloom
    And close their eyes in dread :
  So I, in terror of a fear unknown,
  Untouched by sympathy shall weep alone,
Unless the Hand, which makes the daisies bloom,
    Shall out of kindness raise my drooping head.

Oh ! sun ! Oh moon ! oh ! glitter of star-light
    In canopy of blue !
  Oh ! fragrant breathings of the lungs of morn !
  Oh ! ice-crowned pinnacles,—that proudly scorn
The stifling valleys,—from thy dizzy height
    Entrance me, raise me, into life anew !

Then should I sing as tho' my heart would break
    With joy, out of my woe ;
  For 'tis our sorrow rends from us fine song,—
  Triumphant requiem o'er dead grief and wrong,—
And I would even for sweet sorrow's sake
    Unloose my tongue and sing woe's overthrow.

www.ingramcontent.com/pod-product-compliance
Lightning Source LLC
Chambersburg PA
CBHW030315270326
41926CB00010B/1376